HEAVY MATTERS

A TREATISE ON METAL, MUSIC AND SOCIETY

Bas L.G. Verdin

vzw3-4

CREDITS

Composed by Bas L.G. Verdin MMXIV
www.basverdin.com

Published by vzw3-4 MMXV
Eikenboslaan 19
3010 Kessel-Lo
Belgium

ISBN 978-90-8236-030-1

Copyright MMXV Bas L.G. Verdin & vzw3-4

This book is sold subject to the condition that it shall not, by way of trade or otherwise, be lent, re-sold, hired out, or otherwise circulated without the publisher's prior consent in any form of binding or cover other than that in which it is published and without a similar condition including this condition being imposed on the subsequent purchaser.

The scanning, uploading and distribution of this book via the Internet or via any other means without the permission of the publisher is illegal and punishable by law. Please purchase only authorised electronic editions, and not participate in or encourage electronic piracy of copyrighted materials. Your support of the author's rights is appreciated.

TRACKS

Side A - No easy matter

1. Between the devil and the deep blue sea — 9
2. Senses and senses — 21
3. Metal as music: instruments — 35
4. Metal as music and more: voices — 49

Side B - A matter of time

5. Apollo, Dionysus and other gods — 61
6. Music as media and music as metal — 75
7. Music as metal and the industrial devolution — 87
8. Maps and traps — 99

Thanks to everyone reading everything slowly and legitimately

Side A - No easy matter

1. Between the devil and the deep blue sea

There are two impressions which prompt me to write this treatise. Firstly, that when metal is being discussed, it is seldom being related to fundamental issues. Secondly, when fundamental issues are being discussed, it is seldom being related to metal. Therefore, I am not inclined to write anything close to an encyclopedia on metal for instance. It is typical for an encyclopedia to remain within the framework of so-called facts or data, without thoroughly questioning its subject nor itself. Deeper meanings of a subject remain thereby uncovered and unchallenged. For instance, if one can sum up all of the original band members of Metallica and crew, there is no guarantee at all that this person knows anything about Metallica's music itself. This person could have been born deaf even. On the opposite, I dare to say that it is possible to get the gist of metal, without ever having heard of the name Metallica, nor its music. Say, Rob Halford in 1980 (front man for the older band Judas Priest, called himself Metal God later on). No matter how big the brand Metallica has become, the thing that the young members were doing in some ordinary garage before the name had been invented, is precisely the kind of thing at stake for the writer of a treatise, as well as for the many who have been/are doing such without being addressed by anyone else but an angry neighbour. Even many people who call themselves fans of Metallica or Judas Priest, seem to explore and exhibit every aspect of the b(r)and sooner than the actual compositions, the performing styles, the artistic interrelations, the cultural connotations, the psycho-social mechanisms, the philosophical and religious parallels, etcetera.

However, the use of Metallica as an example of anything, does not go without any problems. While it may help the unexperienced listener and reader to not find herself too alienated from the subject right from the start, it actually does alienate the reader in a certain sense, since metal has become related to Metallica far more among non-metal fans than it has among metal fans. An R&B fan and comrade even asked me once in the beginning: "ah, so you like heavy metallica?". Meaning: you like heavy metal. On the other hand, many a metal fan or metal head makes the distinction between old Metallica and late Metallica, meaning that the old one is real metal and the later one is not. As I am trying to show in this treatise, this and similar matters are far more complex though. But then I might be a head, more than a metal head.

Firstly, before one says that something is not (real) metal, in the latter case for example, one should be able to say what metal is: some sort of a definition that is. Yet, however far I am looking, I am never getting anything that looks remotely like a sound definition, nor even a definition that is not sound. Secondly, the old fan quite obsessively promotes "metal" and her favourite band in all sorts of ways. Yet, when the band finally achieves success indeed, her love suddenly turns into hate? Thirdly, the denouncing ex-fan reveals what we may call a narrow, static and at present conventional opinion about metal music. Yet, how could Kill 'Em All (Metallica's first full-length album, generally having deserved sacred allure in the metal community by now) ever have been created if many a narrow, static and conventional opinion had not been abandoned in the first place? Fourthly, is it more metal then to put on an old Metallica shirt and criticize along safely in the pub so to speak, than to put yourself to playing your own music, with the risk of not getting picked up, if noticed by hoi polloi at all?

Obviously, I do not intend to receive a lot of applause for this treatise. If I would intend so, there are two strategies with high chances of success. More precisely, either to pretend that metal is a simple given, to choose for if you truly belong to the cool ones, and to be trumped by if you do not. Or, to pretend that normal life is a simple given, luckily standing apart from metal, and unluckily being endangered by it. Well, I will not be dissatisfied if both camps disagree with me. For that would prove that a general thinking process has finally started, and that we can lift any mention of metal and the like to a subsequent level at last. A level more profound, dynamic and daring than an encyclopedia, a biography, a self-reclaimed bible, a pro or a contra book. Both all-or-nothing pro and contra positions implicitly claim to have a definition of metal at hand, which they have not. It is an old saying though that one should be silent about what one cannot speak.

So, the camps are far more occupied with endorsing their own tunnel vision than examining the matter concerned. At the same time, they implicitly need each other in order to find their satisfaction as being part of a certain group. The satisfaction thrives precisely on the dualism, of not being the other, rather than on a tested comprehensive philosophy for instance. But why would one be opposed to what one needs? Perhaps because if some would endeavour a tested comprehensive philosophy indeed, the group would eventually come to pieces, and thereby the habitual identification and self-legitimation lost, without a replacement of the same kind.

Nonetheless, this does not mean that we ought to stick by the neutral position, whatever that may be. It is an illusion, and a dangerous one, to be able to be fully neutral. But even if we were able to, I am not convinced that it should be the ending point. Some aspects demand of me a positive reception, others a negative one, still others both positive and negative. Indifference however, would make writing and reading quite pointless. Surely, as many others have already done before me, it is possible to fill a whole treatise with epistemological and ethical concerns as such. If I were to follow this line, the problem here would be that the metal phenomenon would remain what it is: undisputed - undisputed from within. Any general knows that surrounding a city does not mean that the battle has been won. Yes, the walls may seem high, the defenders fierce, but every home keeps a warm fire, and the question is how it is being ignited. Such a question cannot be responded to by questionnaires, neither by literature studies, nor by colonization of the primitives, savages or (metal) race, as we are about to show respectively.

There are many problems with the traditional questionnaire, however popular they seem to be, even in the academic world. Firstly, it is being presupposed that the answer to a question, written or spoken, is the answer being thought, and that the answer being thought is the thing being done. Anyone with an average sense of reality, should know that it is impossible to find someone whose doing or not doing is definitely identical with her thinking or not thinking, with her speaking or not speaking, and her writing or not writing, as if these verbs were all mutually interchangeable. Secondly, the questions themselves are questions from an outsider and his culture. By answering alone, no matter what the answer, one would have to submit to the way of thinking of the other culture instead of her own. Thirdly, having archived all the given answers, does not mean that the most important things about the culture have ever been expressed yet. Not only because the questions are not adequate. Also, because one expresses, verbally or non-verbally, much more and much more important things to an insider than to an outsider. Especially with her allergy to the establishment, it is very likely that the metal head will not be the open book being sought by the established academic in his fancy suit as it were. Questionnaires are often being accompanied by a strict initial research hypotheses to be proven. What else could this mean though than thinking: "we are not eager to be as open as to extensively observe your culture as it comes with all its complexities and initial misunderstandings, but just give us what responds to what we are looking for so we reach our quota, and you will soon be rid of us". Man does not even have all the answers to the original questions of his own culture, so why would he have them for another one's?

Many problems may also occur with a literature study. More pressing than summing them up here, is that there is at this point just hardly any adequate literature available, either about metal, or sprung from the metal culture. A literature study could be very useful when the topic is about writers, or when there is a lot of written experience available from anthropologists among metal heads for instance, but neither is as yet the case. It is most remarkable that a culture both controversial and embraced by so many worldwide as metal, has not been prone to a lively written debate, not even to a small extent. As a matter of speaking, a local group of barely one hundred fans of war hymns in the first half of the twentieth century seems to publish more, than millions of metal fans together across the globe. The Hare Krishna centre around the corner of the street with its dozen of regulars, seems to be studied sooner than the international metal festival coming to town, etcetera. Is this pure coincidence? Logically, either the scholar does not want to study metal, or he is not able to. Either the metal fan does not want to study herself or her peers, or she is not able to.

It is possible to give several reasons for each of the four categories just mentioned. The scholar does not want to, because he might think that the subject is not traditional or decent enough, or that the academic world will think so, or will not provide him with any promotion in any case. The scholar is not able to, because he might never have participated in anything metal, or he does have but lacks understanding, or he does understand but lacks funding, or he lacks promotors who also understand. The metal fan does not want to, because she might want to do easier or other demanding things in her spare time, or she does not prefer to be associated with the school climate, or she wishes to keep everything inside, or she does not see the use of it. The metal fan is not able to, because she might lack sense of self-consciousness, relativism, higher education or uncompensated time. By imagining other reasons still, the question is turning into its opposite: why would one ever consider writing about it at all? Possibly because both the metal fan and the outsider suppose that they understand their respective selves and not the other, whereas writing could expose that they hardly do understand their selves, and getting to understand their selves could encompass getting to understand, therefore not approve of, the other.

Colonists, crusaders, missionaries, evolutionists,... all most interesting to write novels or pieces of music about, but to be rejected as ideals for the cultural observant. In every case, the object is a population supposedly less man than the invader, to be subdued by the supposedly ideal social system at a particular time and place. As if we have had evolution going on, and here and now it is has miraculously stopped at its peak. Metal, or any other (sub)culture (the notion being discussed later on), does not exist without subjects though, and subjects are subjects, not objects. It is so evident that it is often overlooked, but every writer also is a subject, and thus carrier of a certain cultural background, essentially no less curious than the studied "object" itself. All of my methodological concerns above can positively be rephrased as what anthropologists have come to call fieldwork and participant observation.

I said methodological, but it is precisely the point of the latter methodology that methodology and topic are not to be seperated too much. The method is in a certain way the topic itself: to study while standing in the middle of the field, in which we work and relax amongst others who are used to work and relax there, the workers which we study by observing as we are participating, the participants by whom we, on our turn, are being observed, and the at first sight trivial, at other times revealing dynamics which stem from this process, the once misleading signal now meaning something entirely different, in short: the use of the language, and therefore the language itself, in the broadest sense of the word.

Whether it be researchers, composers or other authors, she who wishes to keep up appearances, seems eager to talk about the respective lives of the former relatively more than the actual content of their work. While any author, regardless of his reputation, is a blend of cultural backgrounds, even if he is writing precisely about cultural backgrounds, it is inadequate and often cowardly to talk about the man whose hand it is, instead of the points being written by that hand. This is not to say of course that my points would have been made if none of my participations and observations whatsoever had taken place. An attempt to introduce myself can thus clarify, not replace, the previous and upcoming perspectives put forward in this treatise.

I started and finished to write this treatise at the age of 33, independently and in my spare time, as a sequel to my liquidation of my metal shop, as we will see. I have been told that my birth took place in Leuven, in central Belgium, on 28 October 1980. Hence, I ceased to be dead the winter before. So far, I have always lived in that region, not out of nationalistic feelings of any kind, but plain practical considerations instead. I remember quite a few things from my small years, possibly because what happened for the first time seemed to happen for a lot of times ever after in one way or another. What strikes me most, is that I was thinking back then that people were behaving as they behaved just because they were fellow children or because they were adults only acting like that with children, whereas I discovered only much later that it was primarily because they were ...people as usual.

On the level of studies, I first had to go to school like everybody else, until the year in which we became 18 years old.

That year, I finished at a boys only school with metal bars in front of the windows, in the direction of Latin and ancient Greek - which was about to lose its respectability soon. My conclusions have not really altered: that the most valuable lessons were learned in spite of, rather than thanks to, most teachers and educational policy makers. Also, just in order to respond fairly well to the demands of the tasks set, I had to spend far more than forty working hours a week as a teenager. This was obviously far more than most teachers and educational policy makers spent themselves, and in any case more than is legally considered a healthy amount of obligatory working hours in the twentieth century. Foremost, the time had to be spent ineffectively. Considering that when I went to university afterwards, I had to spend only half of the time in total for similar marks, resulting in more than the double of wisdom. The time won, went especially to making music. Mobiles and computers were no part of our daily lives yet, so I made an awful lot of it.

I officially obtained a Candidate and Licentiate in Philosophy, a Candidate in Social and Political Sciences and a Licentiate in Political Sciences. Notwithstanding, I have always had more of a keen eye on the Humanities in general, consequently making room for possible tensions. To illustrate this: on my final philosophical thesis (say extensive master proof) the judging committee remarked that it was too social scientific, whereas on my final political scientific thesis another committee remarked that it was too philosophical. In fact, they were neither. They were what would as best be called "universital", if we have to label it in the first place. If pieces are not put together, one cannot even tell the difference between a piece and a puzzle, so the puzzle is not likely to ever get solved. Nowadays, many would replace Licentiate by Master, and Candidate by Bachelor. Most Licentiates, including myself, cannot agree with this, since both content and methods underwent, and are still undergoing, severe changes, affecting depth, scope and autonomy of research alike. This is not to say that the status quo would have been perfect. Nor can I agree with the term Science after Social or Political for instance. No, the human world is not as easy as science, and even science itself is much more human than scientific, than is generally assumed. To elaborate on this, would be sufficient material for another treatise.

On the level of work, or much more correctly: a position that is somehow reimbursed for, I have applied for thousands of various jobs, quite literally, without effect. The lesson learned was harsh, but illuminating: that, say, a seven weeks' course on electricity, without any other qualification that appears to be threatening, had been more likely to provide for an income, than seven years of successful surplus study of the above. While these studies entail how to make improvement by thinking in a logical-critical way, employers give the impression to seek quite the opposite: to stagnate by promoting myopia, contradictions and power play - even within universities and public administration. Since it was next to impossible to get a real job, I decided to try to give myself one. That is how I eventually became an independent owner-operator of a physical record shop (CD, LP, DVD,...) specialized in metal music for a handful of years. Both the lasting economic crisis in general and the exponential crisis of the music industry in particular, unfortunately made it look more like a museum than a shop in the end. Since I was not being subsidized like a museum though, quitting was the more sensible path chosen, while I had been combining already with a part-time job.

In the meantime, I had also produced my own mead (honey wine). Most seemed to find it tasteful as well as something they were willing to spend money on, contrary to music, but inflating regulations made it practically impossible for me to carry it out on a professional basis. Apart from being rather hilarious in detail, the regulations make it even theoretically impossible to uphold the traditional and regional ways of producing, and hence the product as such. Administrators, many of whom hidden behind shiny reflecting EU windows, find other issues like thirst and hunger less pressing so it seems, than to abandon the cultural heritage of (honey) wine as our ancestors have developed without significant problems for millennia, when there was little need for the word ecology. Else, I have been working quite a while with an undertaker occasionally. But I have had one or two "normal" jobs with "normal", living people too. Most notably, checking, counting, weighing, scanning and labeling of all possible cargo in all possible ways, and routinely input, copying, piling, passing or holding of accompanying paperwork that was always growing while the personnel was diminishing, framed by Kafka-like procedures, inapt IT and problems of the daily recurring sort, stuffed in a claustrophobic container or confronted with an improvised "desk" in the midst of the antique dust of a loud and either freezing, or hot warehouse, during many a year of evening rush hours by piercing white lights, worn out smelling fluo and inevitable hit radio, in the eyes of capricious managers with a career in flattering "superiors", not even managing their own emotions and ordering to work faster and faster and to ask less and less questions, especially when they concern the substantive enhancement of processes instead of sideshows. Only then, did I realize that I never really understood the Marxist tradition and neo-marxist critical theories before.

In my spare time, I have always been playing plenty of strange sorts of music, as others often call it, that I invented myself alone or with others, on varying instruments and vocals. Originality was never the aim, only the consequence, if I may believe the general perception. My aim has always been simple enough: just a damn fine tune. A couple of hundred gigs, a dozen of self-released albums and plenty more in the closet, being the result. What makes it more comfortable than offstage life, is that you get to form the whole system and carry it out accordingly. Having been expelled from the music academy at the age of 8, due to insubordination to the teacher, or according to myself: subordination to the music, I got to learn everything the alternative way. Around the same age, I decided to get baptized, which happened shortly afterwards. By now, I find myself to have lost that kind of faith, but none of the effort to make sense of this outer world, which alone is already quite an engagement. For about two decades now, I have regularly been into metal related activities. First as a curious explorer, then as a specializing fan and artist, and after my shop experience as a contemplating humanistic all-rounder as it were. While metal has literally only been around for about four decades now, pre-twentieth century culture has also become a core field of interest for me.

In between, I have been a political activist, and have even been a candidate for the elections of our province. Our province had been split when I was a child, into a so-called Dutch (and only

Dutch) speaking part and a so-called French (and only French) speaking part. My mother tongue may happen to be Dutch, but unlike many politicians concerned about that language more than about the little man who speaks it, I have never been in favour of that split. The more I was privileged to have a look into the accustomed ways of doing party politics, the more it became clear to me that the parties were more similar to each other, in pursuing pretty ordinary self-interest in fact, directly or indirectly: the interest of the economically rich, consciously or not: the subordination of art in its diverse forms, and else: way too much steak parties and other hollow *actes de présence* - what has it got to do with politics? - than similar to any grounded ideology whatsoever. Since there was not enough time and means available to convince sufficient people to act otherwise, I withdrew.

So, by witnessing to all this and more, I can only hope to rightfully say one day that I have had the opportunity to be an observing participant/participating observant in many different and difficult worlds, different from each other and yes, different from myself. Or, to put it in a more prosaic way, to be between the devil and the deep blue sea. However, while the expression suggests to having to choose for the one or the other peril, I suggest to definitely not do this. Instead, to try to discover the devil, and how superstition keeps him alive. To try to discover the deep blue sea, and how remaining on the surface keeps it deep.

Some will find these writings not academical enough, others will find them too academical. If this is a result of bringing those worlds closer to each other, we will all have made progress though. Academics have few other options so it seems than either relating metal to something in a way the latter becomes dominant, or selecting one minuscule aspect of it so the global view is being obscured. Additionally, references are primarily being made to other academics instead of, say, metallics, and the writing and reading is primarily being done by academics instead of metallics, thereby creating a vacuum for both negative and positive feedback from the field. Surprisingly enough, the early academics did quite the opposite: while it is nowadays a popular tactics to constantly refer to other academics in order to reap success, the early academic himself, Aristotle for example, did refer to almost nobody or nothing else than the subject as he examined it in person, clearly without any loss of quality, and even with an added value I would add.

Metallics have few other options so it seems than leaving no room for anything other than metal, either by not integrating it in a larger view, or by not disintegrating it. Additionally, the informal references they make are primarily taken for granted, instead of explained to the outer and even inner world, thereby creating another vacuum for reflective criticism or support. Again, making a lot of common references has become an easier way to score in the community, than developing or reinventing the subject as if they were the early metallics themselves. No, we have abundant other options. I might be choosing an unusual one, but it only is just one of the many.

2. Senses and senses

"Metal is a hard substance such as iron, steel, copper, or lead. ...pieces of furniture in wood, metal and glass... He hit his head against a metal bar. See also base metal." Surprisingly or not, that is all my thick English dictionary has got to tell about "metal". Even though I have used the word in my previous writings with virtual comfort, I am quite sure that the reader had some sort of a meaning in mind. And leaving aside whether the meaning was right or wrong, I am as sure that it had nothing to do with the sense in the dictionary.

Two points may already catch our attention. Firstly, that a meaning grasped and named by so many, even outside the English speaking parts of the world, by the name of metal, is not being mentioned in the good old dictionary. Perhaps there is, or will be, a dictionary that describes what we are trying to say when we are saying metal in a not-chemical way, but this is as yet nothing that we can rely on. Secondly, if I were to bet on which of the meanings of metal is being meant more often, if we were able to pile up every mention of the word around the world on a common day, I would bet on the meaning not being meant in my dictionary. Not only because there are at this moment quite likely less fans of chemistry than fans of metal, but also because it is a key factor for fans of metal to relate to the word metal itself as much and as articulate as possible. Much more than chemists anyway, who would at once relate to the particular sort of metal, and much more than fans of jazz for instance concerning their genre, who would rather do some chemistry while listening to jazz than scream out "Jazz!!!" all of a sudden in the middle of the street so to speak. Metal fans do scream out "Metal!!!" quite expressively, accommodated by some gesticulations, especially the "devil's hand" by stretching the index and little finger and closing the middle finger and ring finger. It is relatively less, but also widespread to shout a metal band name on a regular basis, without anything about that band even being present, most remarkably the "Slayer!!!" hype. I have never known someone shout "Miles Davis!!!" though, unless he must have been around of course.

In this way, the good news is that there is a lot of room left for interpretation of metal. The bad news is that there is hardly any explicit interpretation of it. Perhaps someone wrote it in her diary someday, but then again: it is not common. I cannot stress enough that common belief, defenders and offenders alike, tends to pretend exactly the other way around: that there is almost no room left for interpretation and, as a consequence, that there is a settled interpretation. In other words, they act like our meaning of metal being point of focus here, has been in the dictionary unchanged and unchallenged for ages. Of course, it is not the first time in history that a thing like this happens. For instance, before the written word was being pressed, people tended to think that the Earth was flat and at rest. It took a lot of underground writing, pressing and reading to argue otherwise, and if a Copernicus had not lived so close in time to a Gutenberg, it is quite possible that we still would generally believe that the Earth is not round and moving. Writing has the potential to force the reader but also the writer herself to reflect, correctly or incorrectly. Who wants to avoid confrontations though, starts to avoid writings. As such, both reflection and development is hindered to take place.

Hence, let us continue: while the metal we are talking about has, strictly speaking, nothing to do with chemistry, it considerably helps to start disentangling the concept in a chemical way. None withstanding that seeing my personal memoirs, this is rather ironic. Teachers found my approach unacceptable particularly in chemistry and aesthetics. When I am writing that metal is mostly part of aesthetics, and is in a certain sense to be studied the chemical way, this clearly must be a sign of hubris. Admittedly, but then the easiest way is not always the best way, and definitely not in this case.

By chemistry, I mean in no particular order, firstly, dividing one thing into plural things, secondly, connecting certain divisions to each other, thirdly, connecting certain divisions to one thing, fourthly, connecting certain divisions or one thing to other things, fifthly, connecting the resulting dynamics to time and space (which are also mutually connected, following Albert Einstein). Concretely and respectively, dividing metal into plural things, connecting certain divisions of metal to each other, to metal and to other things than metal, and to connect it to space-time. Precisely by doing so, the matter proves to be more heavy to catch than it may appear. Whereas chemistry is about substances, metal is about mental things. Only one letter different, but it makes a big difference. And whereas metal in the chemical sense is a substance, it is not so in the aesthetic sense, otherwise chemistry would have to be considered a substance too.

This is not to say two things. Firstly, while metal is about mental things indeed, it seems to be quite possible that such a mental thing favours a substantialist concept of metal, which I do not defend, waiting for a fixed definition still. In comparison, God can be believed in as a godly substance, even though it is not being considered this or that piece of wood for instance. In an animistic world view however, God is indeed in the piece of wood, but then he is also in the piece of iron etcetera, so there is no substantialism in the mental way, even though there is substance in the material way. Secondly, by the above I do not mean that a dualism needs to exist of material things on the one hand and ghostly things on the other hand, nor do I mean that a monism needs to exist. I merely mean that the chemist laborates with a bunch of fluids for instance, instead of a bunch of metal heads Whether metal heads consider themselves phenomenological existentialists or not, that does not matter for the time being: they just stand in the world in a way that fluids do not.

Therefore, the question "what is the metal head?" needs to be replaced by the question "who is the metal head?". Again, as the metal head does not appear anywhere in my official dictionary, I have been chewing on the term in its common sense meaning. With almost childish naivety do I declare that the metal head neither appears anywhere in my world. Naturally, I have bumped into an abundance of metal heads at many times at many places, but I have never bumped into "the" metal head. And I know nobody who ever has. It is possible that our senses deceive us, but if they do, I had better lay this treatise aside again, never to be completed. Instead, I do believe that we can rightfully say that "the" metal head does not exist, because nothing has given us reason whatsoever yet to even consider its existence. So, the question needs to be replaced by "who are metal heads?".

Metal heads are humans. Animals, devils, plants, angels,... some might indeed look like them, but closer analysis indicates that they are not. Humans have senses, sometimes working, at other times not, but always five: hearing, seeing, smelling, tasting and feeling. And healthy humans behave themselves or they do not, a certain behaviour they have. What they do or not, what happens between their ears making sense or nonsense that makes them to, what comes into their ears,... as simple the questions, as multiple the answers.

Hearing, so I began to sum up. When certain metal music is being played, a variety of human reactions is possible, going from the one extreme to the other. For instance: "that is not music", "that is not good music", "I do not find that good", "that is good, but not my thing", "that is my thing", "that is the end". In the first case, it is literally being considered: not, or not even partly, music. In the last case, it can be considered: part of good music, that is even part of something bigger.

In the worst case, the listener obviously does not like, or does pretend to obviously not like, what she is hearing. But does that mean that it is not music? Does one ever say, when tasting a whisky for instance: "that is not music"? No matter how correct that would be, I did not think so. As a matter of fact, one only seriously says "that is not music", concerning things that fall anywhere within the scope of audio qualities qualified by humans in a way animals do not seem able to and some humans seem anxious about: as music. Some people, in the vain of John Cage, consider even the audio signals only inadvertently produced by the audience upon the silence produced by the artist, as music. None such difficult cases present yet in metal though.

So, a multitude of things are music, and music is a multitude of things. Easy enough, yet so easily forgotten. It is actually very odd when people say, and they do that a lot, that they like music, without further notice, without saying good music for instance, or what they find good music. As if he who likes music, likes any music, which is a multitude indeed. Mostly, it occurs to me precisely the opposite way: that the dedicated music lover is more difficult to please than the amateur, so that he likes general music in fact less than an average person, and only particular music far more. Pretty much the same with movies for instance: the more you passionately dig into it, the less you just take any movie on the television as it comes, and the more variety in the ways of liking. Simply put: who likes everything, loves nothing. A promising working title also to relate to so-called social media, like Facebook, but that would require yet another treatise.

Concerning my shop, I give away though that there was an overall inverse relation between online liking and offline buying. A possible explanation is that either these were "friends" on other grounds who never really took the effort to find out what the music actually is about without willing to accentuate that they do not care, or these were (wannabe) metal heads using the media to give (false) evidence of their metal membership. The fact that in the endless cyber labyrinth everything is made "my profile", my "selfie", my this and my that, proves precisely that the need for personal recognition is as increasing as unanswered though. If there is nothing happening in real life, then the recognition will also not be real. The only thing that is real is the infringement of the principles of authenticity, privacy and intellectual property. That there were even companies entering my door to propose to increase the number of likes for me, in exchange for royal compensations, underlines the nonsensical, not only because the representation of a world is becoming more important then than the world itself, but also because the more people get conditioned by cyber demands, the less they seem to understand the worth of music and other arts that the few who are not fully conditioned yet, try to establish with all their scarce time, money and energy. At the same time, the means are becoming more important than the content. When someone found out that I played music, the impetuous response was: "How cool! So, you have films on YouTube and such?". When my answer was negative, but that I had a full album of it in my pocket and a nearby gig in the following month, her initial enthusiasm had been cooled down to zero.

Back to our reactions, when people say "that is not music", as well as the decisive, denigrating and agitated tone with which it is usually being said, they express at the most that they really, really do not wish to approve publicly of the thing being heard, its producers and its proponents, even though that thing actually is some sort of music, that can be studied by musicologists. By doing so, any musicological discussion is being abandoned altogether. In order to not having to defend herself with any musicological arguments, all one has to do is to tell it is not about music, or so it seems. Theoretically, the displeased here does her best to keep the concept of metal away from the concept of music. As a consequence, asking about her understanding of metal will not result in any musicological insights, nor in any insights in whisky tasting as we examined above, and so forth. Alternatively, the signals sent and received, heard but not listened to, bear a sociological or psychological undertone.

When the piece of metal music is considered "the end" however, the listener does not always just want to express that he really, really approves of the piece of music as music. Sometimes the music is considered fundamental for his ...being. This means that the hearing can be related to the hearing indeed, say the good or the bad music, but also to the non-hearing: the original, attractive or repulsive condition of being. Call it an experience of depth, both deep inside and transcending the aesthetic piece, representing the notions of beauty/ugliness, good/evil, truth/lie,... themselves as it were. Of course, it is also possible to relate the non-hearing to the hearing in far less spiritual ways. Let us recall the human senses, conduct and mind. Like any music, metal music can be related to the vision, for instance black, related to the tasting, for instance beer, to the smelling, for instance fire, and to the sensing, for instance eroticism.

Of course, the distinctions are at times more theoretical than practical, and spillovers, mutual, and to and from the behaviour and ways of thinking, are ample. Black can literally become the colour you are wearing all of the time, and it can figuratively become your basic view on the world. Beer can get used or abused, as a way to encourage your free-thinking or to discourage your thinking as such in support of the feeling, the lines not being that definite always and everywhere. Fire can be sit by as your favourite smell and idea of cosiness and authenticity, and it can at the very same time be worshipped as a symbol or even tool for your destructive and/or constructive appetites. Eroticism can become a liberal cultivation of the natural effect of attraction, and it can become a libertarian purpose on itself maximizing the senses and the power with disrespect of the other and oneself. All put together, the black T-shirt can depict a band logo under which a metal fan having a voluminous beer poured out by a likewise topless waitress in the one hand, and the remote control to put the bank opposite the terrace on fire in the other hand. A fictional, I think, but very realistic example, like there can be found by the dozens.

It should be clear that wearing such a shirt does not mean putting the depiction itself into practice, any more than that the depiction of a crucified man, be it Jesus Christ or not, tells us anything about the person in possession of the depiction being in favour of the death penalty or not. A metal head need not have a criminal record for instance in order to be considered metal by his peers, even though displaying such a shirt would indeed be considered a crime by jurisdiction of some countries still. Neither need a criminal advocate metal in order to be considered criminal. Luckily enough, or a lot of crime would go unpunished. My point is not that a metal fan would be more criminal or less than a techno fan or a folk fan, only that a wide range of extremities and boundaries in life and death, whatever they may be, are considerably given attention in the metal world hereby (re)created.

Even though I wish not to examine here whether there might be found some correlation at a certain time and place, not to be confused with causal relation, between musical genres and criminality, my very personal experiences indicate that there is, for me, a negative correlation between metal and, say, negative forces. More clearly: the more I can ventilate or "channel" negative forces by the harmless practice of metal, the less inclination to do some real harm afterwards. For the very same reason, I am always surprised when parents are making so much effort to prevent their children from playing violent computer games for instance. Is it not better to be violent in a game or in dreamland, than on the street? To judge people on grounds of their thoughts instead of their deeds, that seems to me more likely though to become the practice of criminality and even totalitarianism: "you actually did not do anything wrong, but still you are condemned to lifetime imprisonment, because we think that you once thought about doing this or that". And to deny that one has ever negative thoughts herself, is in itself probably more an immoral act, namely the act of lying to the others and herself, than any proof of any virtue. All this even supposing negative and positive are so very easily discernible. A similar mechanism might be at work when James Hetfield (front man for Metallica) tells us that without his music, he would have been dead or in prison.

Yes, a handful of policemen entered my metal shop once, in their uniforms, but it was only to order the new release of an extreme metal band. Yes, I did once, and only once, notice a metal head had been stealing from my shop, but when I experimented with making it a theme on social media, reactions went into the direction that it is not metal to steal. Let it be noted: they did not mention that it was not moral, for that would probably imply a relation to the society seen as conformist and organized criminal, but that it was not metal. Yes, metal heads can wear arm and wrist bands with pins you can get hurt by, yet the only time when someone excused himself if he had inadvertently stepped on my toes at a crowded festival, it was precisely a guy with long pins all over the body. Yes, metal might be associated with evoking disobedient behaviour, but when I asked the prison nearby if I could give a concert there with my folky solo-project, the response of the manager was: "too bad it is not metal".

Agreed or not, the metal imagery seems to be provocative and provoking. What I find more remarkable, is that it is being thought that way both by senders of the imagery and receivers of the communication alike. Senders, possibly thinking: "we conforming? this will teach you!", receivers thinking: "how improper! will you ever grow up?". Philosophers amongst us might be thinking though: "you both claiming to think? will both of you ever grow up?". Since, philosophically speaking, the imagery can in fact be seen as a material form. In this way, any fuss about the imagery actually reveals mere display of materialism. If materialism is a degradation of human thinking, to grow up should on the contrary mean to let materials matter less and arguments and actions matter more. The philosopher might have found another striking element. Suppose a metal man who thinks he is being nonconformist, and his society is being conformist. If that is so, then why is he obviously trying to look so hard like the other metal men? In other words, why is he trying to be conformist? As we have pointed out, this does not necessarily make the position of the conformist non-metal men any less problematic. If the norm being conformed with entails superficial materialism, is that something to be conformed with in the first place? Moreover, if the norm being conformed with actively or passively entails "conformism is good and nonconformism bad", is that not a form of hollow circular reasoning not to base any society or identity on?

For now, it suffices that these examples show that the sense of metal which we are talking about, is not a fait accompli, even if it were in the dictionary. As ample the human capabilities, encompassing both literal and figurative senses of sensing, feeling and thinking, as ample the forms of culture in general, and metal in particular. As ample also the forms of music culture, as ample the forms of metal music, which will be continued later. Let us reconsider the hearing aspect of metal music. I have been witness to an abundance of instances wherein people said "I do not like metal", in a less, but still, confusing way reformulated here as "I do not like metal music". Likewise, I have made myself unpopular an abundance of instances by asking back to sum up only ten metal bands, metal records, tunes they have heard, or whatever. Knowing that the quite acclaimed online Encyclopedia Metallum - The Metal Archives, even considered by some to focus on a too narrow understanding of metal music, enlists about 100.000 metal bands as I write, and counting, this clearly cannot be too much to ask. Yet, I am still waiting for most of the responses. This means that people can claim to not like certain music, even if they have no clue about that certain music.

This, on its turn, definitely does not mean that giving ten correct answers to my question above, resolves the confusion. The reason being as simple as important: the kind of metal music known by those who know very little of it, say outsiders, seems to be miles away in most cases from the kinds of metal music insiders deem representative. I am not saying that this is a problem only for metal music. The same might be true for what we call classical music, not that I am an expert in this field, once we understand that classical music can be considered both the umbrella term and a specific era of the genre for example. Likewise, if outsiders of classical music are asked to give ten references, either these tend to cover only the best-sellers of the classical sub genre on their streaming list titled Christmas or relaxation for instance, or these actually belong to other eras without them being aware of the differentiation or interrelation of those sub genres, not to mention less exploited composers of the classical sub genre itself. Unlike classical music however, libraries have been quite empty and therefore useless when it comes down to finding any clarification of metal as music or even metal as such. Since one cannot understand metal without metal music, and since metal music is very rarely studied, not to mention understood, this is something that we will have to compensate for in the sections to follow.

So far, we have been using the words knowing and liking without explicit distinction. Mathematically speaking, it is possible, firstly, to know something and to like it, secondly, to know something and to not like it, thirdly, to not know something and to like it, and fourthly, to not know something and to not like it. The third possibility might be counter-intuitive, yet there seem to be quite a few who like the exotic, without them really knowing how this or that other world actually is, for the love of exoticism itself who knows, and it is quite possible that they would not like it so much once they knew it better, moving then to category two. As we have indicated above, it does not occur that often though that people do not know metal music, yet intend to like it, thereby remaining in category four. More remarkably even, I find it very hard to find someone from category two: someone who knows metal music very well, yet does not like it at all. As a consequence, these categories are populated most: to not know metal music and to not like it, or to know metal music and to like it.

Within the latter, another important distinction is to be distilled. Interestingly enough, it is possible to be a connoisseur of metal music, and a more or less secret admirer of the genre, without getting into the visual, behavioural or ideological forms associated with the genre other than accidentally. Indeed, it is possible to be concerned about metal as music, in the same way as it is possible to be concerned about music as metal. The other way around, it is even possible to look and act like a metal fan from top to toe, from the cradle to the grave, without having a serious understanding of the musical aspects of the metal genre or genres.

Contrary to spontaneous belief, plenty of observations of mine add to this. Out of the ten most buying customers of metal music in my shop, there were more customers that would not particularly be noticed as being a metal fan, if you were to pass them by on the street, than customers that live by a metal dress code. At the same time, people entering the shop giving a metal appearance in any possible way, were relatively more likely to just look at the albums instead of pre-listening, buying or discussing them. When we had the occasion to talk then, it was indeed relatively more difficult to start talking about the music of metal itself, than about merchandise, which is the term in the metal world generally used for all kinds of band clothing and the like, or about metal parties for instance. It seemed even not exceptional to proudly wear logos of bands, whose music the bearer did not have in his collection, did not know by heart or did not know at all. Resulting even in some unintentionally putting on logos in the wrong direction: on their heads. I would especially not have been able to imagine this scene: a mother walks in and asks for metal clothes for her son who will be attending a metal festival, because, I quote, he has to look proper - as if the poor boy was going to apply for a job and needed a costume.

No matter how hard to understand, it could be explained like this: who looks like a metal fan most, spends all her money on window-dressing, hanging out and beer for instance, so there is no money left for the music, or, she lives less with her ears so to speak than with her other senses, or, the drive to belong to the (metal) community is stronger than the drive to be into appealing (metal) music, or visual arts are simply valued more than audio arts, etcetera. Two important refinements. Firstly, whereas I generally use "she/her" and "he/him" only to vary accidentally, out of feminist concerns let us say, in this particular case it might be suit in a certain sense, since women as an average have proven to buy far less metal music than men do, even though they are nowadays getting represented in the world of metal appearance quite well. Secondly, to point out that the correlation between acting like a metal fan and being a fan of metal music is far from being necessary in either direction, especially when we examine both extremes, does not mean that there is not some sort of a blend of the two in most cases, with or without the fans themselves being aware of that.

Still, things appear to be easier than they actually are. But then the word music is as simplifying as the word metal. The problem is that there is not really a singular or plural form at hand. As if music would exist if there were no "musics", and as if metal would exist if there were no "metals". However far-fetched it may appear, its relevance is not to be missed. Let us suppose that we meet someone who says "I like metal music". Of course, having been the man at the bar of a metal music shop, there was plenty occasion. The odd thing is now, that when we started extensive listening sessions, the metal fan seemed to be highly picky. There seemed to be even more records he did not want to have, than records he did want to have. Also, after some more sessions, it became clear to me that the fan maintained a certain pattern in his liking. Some patterns were simple, some complex, some could easily be described, for instance as the headliners of a certain sub genre, the monthly top so much of a specialized magazine or the line-up of this or that festival, others being less easy, but therefore not less discernible. Two customers, both claiming to like metal and metal music alike, could easily prove to choose inexplicitely for very different such patterns. When I had the occasion to meet both customers at the same time, the one would not even refrain from making public his spontaneous disdain for the choice of the other, in my eyes equal, metal fan. In other words, when it comes down to it, the metal fans display less unity on musical grounds than they otherwise suggest with regard to themselves and the others, which is not to say that other grounds should be impossible.

 I, for my part, learned a different but similar point: the more I have been able to dig into metal, either by examining a field of my own choice, or by being put in a situation to having to search and do research in a certain direction, the harder it became to postulate the unity of it all. The otherwise plain saying of old, seems to be bare some truth in this case at least: the more you know, the less you know. As I have been explaining, and will continue to explain, the metal phenomenon would appear more simple than it is, if we did not make a distinction between metal and metal as music, as well as distinctions within metal as music itself and within metal as, say, lifestyle. Even more complicating, one can be a fan of the same phenomenon, out of many thus within the metal phenomenon, for varying reasons. For instance, the same metal band can be hailed by the one for its high speed, by the other for its catching melodies, by another for its lyrical themes, artwork or styling, by yet another for its historical meaning, controversial status or simply popularity, and so forth.

The audio-focused material is what we are going to investigate further for starters, by many overlooked in their explicit or implicit bias against metal, by many overlooked in their anxious strive for being part of the place-to-be where it is happening on a social level instead of what is happening on a musical level, only by some rightfully taken seriously as a Pandora's box of climaxes both in and of music history. As stated before, I am not a musicologist, but since there seems no appropriate and up to date work available yet to just refer to, we are to initiate it by ourselves.

The least misleading of few attempts is probably "Running with the Devil: Power, Gender, and Madness in Heavy Metal Music" by Robert Walser. The problems however, that it has been written over twenty years ago and is missing more than half of metal's core development both in time and place, that the story is too good/neglects some important disturbing elements, and that it never reached outside the academic sphere. I am not saying that the current attempt is a better one, only a different one.

3. Metal as music: instruments

Paradoxically, metal musicians in general tend to look less metal in daily life than their die hard fans. Metal music is indeed much more than meets the eye. Musical instruments have to be made, studied and practiced. Vocals have to be amplified, developed and integrated. Compositions, lyrics and artwork have to be noted, put together and materialized. Recordings have to be prepared, executed and paid for. Concerts have to be sought, driven to and accomplished. Bands have to be managed, produced and promoted. The to do list is never finished.

Since metal bands very rarely have got the luxury for instance to be included in the overall hit parade, they cannot depend on the success they once had with a hit or two containing two minutes and thirty seconds, and they need to keep on working, constantly. Mainly on top of the regular job they have besides, having nothing to do with their rather voluntary job as a musician. This counts even for the bigger bands in the genre, especially now intellectual property and autonomy has lost its respect. Another subject for another book. As we have indicated above, the bands are nonetheless very numerous, which makes the competition very hard, which makes them having to work even harder. As we are about to tell, the music itself demands thereby a tremendous effort, all of which makes putting together a metal band almost seem like a masochistic activity. Not to mention finding capable, willing and disciplined band members in the neighbourhood in the first place.

I remind that this treatise has no ambition whatsoever to be a complete metal manual. So, someone starting to read from this section, on a website I have not authorized for example, in case she is about to write a paper on metal music in Wikipedia style, better stops and starts reading from the beginning of this treatise, or gather her own findings of course, in which case however the deadline for the paper will not likely be met. Not only is it an illusion that metal is something complete, definite and finished. Also, the things seldom being said are quite often the things most significant. My ambition is merely to let aspects of metal see daylight, which do not as a rule catch the attention of outsiders and even insiders, and which are nonetheless important for a fair, balanced and comprehensive approach of metal.

Metal bands can take many forms. A quite normal metal band would consist of a drummer, a bass guitar player, two guitar players and a singer. The singer can be separate indeed, but can be at the same time a guitar player, or, less occurring, a player of bass guitar or another instrument. In case the singer is one of the guitar players, he usually plays the rhythm guitar, while the other guitar player plays the lead guitar, meaning playing more solos and variations on the basic themes - if metal themes are ever basic. Backing vocals from one till all band members are not required but ample. More than one lead singer is not that usual, but it happens. Not in the sense that there would be an entire choir, which has however been done also, but that there are mostly two contrasting singers then. For instance, the combination of a male and a female singer. The instruments are mostly occupied by men. In the early days the vocals as well, but female vocalists keep gaining field as we speak.

When there is talk of a solo metal band, it is usually being meant in the way that there is one man who plays, programs and/or delegates all instruments, instead of there being one man playing one instrument with one line as such. If the latter should occur, a folk metal fusion for example might be apt though, in the vein of some of Ice King's works. When there is talk of an orchestral metal band, it is not primarily being meant in the way that there would be a London symphonic orchestra for instance with metal as its regular repertoire. Combination projects of a metal band and an orchestra are surely no exception though, but then there is the band at the one hand and the orchestra at the other hand. Again, I am not declaring that exceptions are absent, or that it needs to be that way, but mostly such seems to be as yet the case in common practice. Also, it can be meant that the band plays orchestral or symphonic metal music, even though there is no orchestra at play, but just the handful of band members say.

Other instruments than those put forward above are definitely not out of the question. The more metal evolves, the more other instruments seem to be incorporated even. Keyboards have been relatively the most popular for a long time though, by now added with or replaced by computer modulating, sampling and programming of all sorts. Else, one could easily cover a whole page mentioning other instruments. Most important is to know that a wide variety can be found, both from the electronic and the acoustic spectre, both from old and new cultures, both from the north and the south, etcetera.

Either, other instruments are being used to accompany the basic setting of the band here and there, in a decorative way so to speak. Or, the "special" instrument(s) is/are even decisive for the overall sound of the band, and the brand in this case. Let it be noted though that there is no general appreciation or depreciation of this. Some find it a welcome widening or deepening of the sound, while others prefer core business with the electric guitars, drums and vocals. Some think metal music is growing as it is expanding its boundaries, while others think that it is shrinking as it is being contaminated. I do not think it is cowardly to not decide about this matter actually. For whoever thinks about metal in terms of music, as we are doing right now, will find it more important how the music calls him, than how he calls the music.

Concerning the playing itself of an instrument, I would guess that the member of a metal band is in general more able to, therefore not willing to, play the part of a member of a pop band, than vice versa. The reason being simple: to be able to play an average piece of metal music as it is to be played, requires a relatively highly advanced playing technique. No matter how much someone dislikes the content of an average piece of metal music, she has to give metal musicians this at least: most of them know very well how to play and how to put into practice what they know. Yet, the compliment is hardly ever being given. The best way to prove this, is to challenge everyone to try to create or imitate an "average" metal piece they like or dislike. It is my experience that even academically trained musicians have to do a great deal of study first.

Consequently, this could be an explanation why metal music is seldom being taught through the official educational channels. It is mostly just too difficult to start with for the pupil, or perhaps to end with for the teacher. Instead, easy tunes from a commercial television program for children are being taught for instance. That is at least how I can remember it. Thus, not only do metal musicians play a lot of difficult parts, also they would not have been able to, if they did not have a huge amount of self-discipline to try to learn it outside the standard channels given by society, and, no less important, outside their daily societal tasks. No matter how noisy someone might find a particular piece of metal music, it is in about all instances in fact extremely ordered, and executed accordingly. The kind of noise that you get when you put people together who cannot play, is of a very different kind. Of course, when someone has not got a lot of musical talents, she will find it difficult to discover order in any music other than childish chorus, repetitive beat, muzak, or music that is designed to just make the silence disappear.

A similar paradoxical element is to be discerned. People seem to prefer to do small talk when the background sound provides for music of the easy listening sort. When the background sound provides for metal music, the word noise might spring from their lips. As a matter of fact, precisely because there is more to listen to and more musical order in the latter case, the talking becomes more difficult and spoils both the conversation and the music. In other words, things become noisy more when you combine background noise (talking) with non-noise (intensive music), than when you combine background noise (talking) with background noise (plain easy music).

Before we go into details concerning some typical playing techniques in metal, one might try to counter-argue that a band like Nirvana is technically not demanding at all. It has indeed been common practice here to imitate Nirvana when one starts learning how to play the guitar. Even though the imitations are rather poor most of the time, the music itself is quite simple really. There are a lot of clarifying nuances to be made though. A scout, knowing that the band has been so popular among scouting groups here, seems to be pleased with just playing their songs over and over again, while a metal fan seems to work his way through this phase, hoping to play one day something like Yngwie J. Malmsteen for instance. Who does not know Malmsteen, should know two things for now: that he plays a technically too high level for most players, even metal players, no matter how experienced they get, and that his music is considered much more metal among metal fans than Nirvana is among metal fans. It is ironic that Malmsteen himself does not wish to be labeled as a metal band though, seeming to prefer to be the straight successor of the baroque tradition. Nirvana would be considered part of the genre grunge, much more than metal, even though outsiders tend to mix it all up. There has even been a serious tension between grunge in general and metal. Among metal fans, it is often being said, rightly or wrongly, that the eighties were the good years for metal, and the nineties bad years, since it had to give ground to "grunge and such". There were even quite a lot of reputed metal bands, who saw themselves forced to make their complex eighties sound more easy, worldly and grungy in the nineties. Even though this sometimes helped to gain fans among people who otherwise do not listen to metal so much, most metal fans were not pleased with this. I myself do not tell this to create any bias against grunge, but the case helps to get into the head of the metal head Also, I would point out that most grunge bands other than Nirvana are far less simple than them.

Shortly put, in music you have the piece of music and the way it is being played. At least in theory, because the two are practically interrelated: in order to play a certain piece, you need to play in a certain way, and in order to play in a certain way, you need a certain piece. Even though the distinction between metal and rock music is not the same for everyone, many pieces in metal music cannot be played or composed while sticking to basic rock techniques and methods.

Let us consider the metal drums first. Of course, I do not mean that the drums are made of metal, even though some parts are, but the set-up of the drum kit in metal music and how it is being used. Even someone who does not know anything about drumming, would notice that a drum kit in metal music is just much bigger most of the time than a drum kit anywhere else. This is not to say that in other genres extensive drumming is not possible, but this tends to be due then either to multiple drummers instead of only one, for instance tribal, or to extensive use of less drumming equipment by only one drummer, for instance jazz. Also, this is not to say that the particular drums are directly bigger, but that the drum kit itself is more extensive. As a consequence however, this means that more variety occurs within the drum kit, resulting in both bigger and smaller drums and cymbals as otherwise usual.

Probably the most distinctive feature of metal drumming, and a distinctive feature of metal music as such, to a somewhat lesser extent the hard rock family, is the double bass drum. Imagine a right-handed drummer with two feet. In other music, the left foot would be used for the hi-hat, to lift or drop with a pedal the upper of two cymbals, adversely fixed on respectively a sliding bar within a static bar. The right foot would be used to hit the bass drum with a pedal with a relatively soft stick. This is the drum meeting the ground on it side, with the biggest skins and therefore the lowest frequency, making a relatively short sound when hit. Well, most metal drummers use two of them at the same time, either by having two separate bass drums, or by having double pedals for one bass drum, in case of lack of space or funds. So, one bass drum pedal for every foot. Consequently, this may limit the dynamics of the hi-hat, but since metal drummers also use many cymbals, this can be compensated for by hitting other cymbals with a similar effect with the hand sticks. The combined bass drumming has a major effect though, only to a certain extent comparable to traditional marching bands, who use two hand sticks for the same bass drum however. The succession of the basses in staccato allow for maximum tempo, maximum rhythm and maximum power all at once. Due to this system, the whole drum experience gets different, both for the audience and the player. Thereby, it is clear that it is anything but evident to be able to drum tightly with double bass. When played at a high volume, it gets even hard to distinguish between the reflecting of the sound of the bass drums on your chest and your own heartbeat, so the effect should not be underestimated.

An important remark. Double bass has been used in a different meaning, long before the word metal music or even rock and roll had been invented, as a very large contrabass that is. The most impressive of them all, the octobass, was invented right in the middle of the 19th century by Jean-Baptiste Vuillome. It even took two people to play it. Even though this is part of the string instruments, instead of percussion, one can imagine that the intention must have been quite similar: to create more bombast, variety and extremity. In other words, to make music more heavy. Heavy metal, or not.

In the same way, metal drummers who have enough place and means, buy two or even more floor toms, instead of the regular one. The floor tom is the lowest of the toms to be hit with a stick in the hand, both in frequency and position, as it is standing on the floor, to the right for the right-handed. Multiple floor toms can of course create another heavy effect, from the orchestral and the theatrical to the ritualistic and the military. The frequency and position of the other toms display great variety. To the left, standing above the hi-hat and even before that, extremely small toms are set-up, accompanied by toms always getting a little bigger to the right, thus making the circle almost complete to the floor toms. Sometimes the circle is even complete, so the drummer has got to move something first before he can leave his drum kit. The wide range of frequencies allows for excessive fill-ins from high to low and back again, say the variations upon or in between the basic rhythm, the distinction between the two thereby getting blurred. Evidently, a lot of regular drummers, who have only one or two toms, one floor tom and one bass drum, cannot do this, and put more attention to the basic rhythm, instead of what we might call maximalistic rhythm. For the same reason, the latter rhythm encompasses more melodic aspects: it becomes possible to play a tune instead of merely a rhythm.

In many musical genres, the snare drum plays a crucial role in defining the rhythm and tempo of a piece. It is the drum placed in between the knees of the drummer, whether or not she plays with double bass drum. The snares can be put against the lower skin of the drum, producing its characteristic sound when hit, making many an eye blink because of the combination of loud and short. In metal music, the snares are almost always put on. Sometimes an additional snare drum is set up. In many musical genres, the snare drum almost sounds like being played by an automatic pilot so to speak, because of its striking regularity throughout the piece, and in electronic applications this is often even true. For two reasons, this is less so in metal music. Not only does the tempo witness relatively a lot of changes within one song, because the song consists of multiple parts with their own tempo, making it quite a challenge in many cases to set a metronome. Also, the scope of tempo is relatively wide: everything between and on the borders of very slow and very fast, and sometimes even too fast for the standard analogue metronome. Most metal fans prefer hard, fast and tight hitting of the snare drum, thereby increasing the "attack factor", above brushing for instance, as would rather be welcomed in jazz.

Percussion parts of all sorts also find their way into the drum kit of the metal player, along with undefined parts that the drummer made himself, by combining or creatively destructing things. And, I guess the cymbal producing industry would be in crisis if there were no metal drummers, for two reasons. Not only because a lot of different cymbals are being used by one metal drummer, but also because they are being used so intensively that they get broken sooner. Of course, the same counts for drum sticks, skins, and so forth. For the same reason, it is even more problematic than it already is, to listen to metal music online. The diminished quality of the online sound, can by most people best be heard while listening to the cymbals. As cymbals are more represented in metal, the online loss of quality should be more clear in metal. Or, positively put, the original is in metal much more qualitative than one would think.

We might conclude here that it is hard to get to know the face of the drummer of a metal band, as he is hidden behind his drum kit. Not hidden in the sense that you would not notice if or what he plays, but in the opposite sense: that he plays so much, that the drums seem to even literally absorb him. If you do see him, you would rather think he is a sportsman though, wearing often not more than a pastel boxer's shirt and ditto sweatband. Indeed, remarkably contrasting with the heavy formal clothing of his band members. But then, without being sportive, it is just impossible to play the drums as it is generally being expected in metal.

Secondly, the guitars. In metal music, guitars are almost always electric guitars. Acoustic guitars would be more difficult for two reasons. Not only would they have to be amplified in an electric way, to be able to compete with the naturally high volume of the acoustic drums. Also, acoustic guitars are less compact than electric guitars, which means that difficult parts, being ample in metal music, can be executed more handy and stimulated more by electric guitars. Probably the most distinctive feature of metal guitars, and of metal music as such, is the abundant use of so-called distortion effects. An effect is an adaptation of the sound coming directly from, in this case, the electric guitar. Effects can adapt but maintain the naturally clean sound of the guitar, for instance by echo or reverb, or they can roughen it as it were, by overdrive or, more extremely, distortion. While a clean sound often occurs in folk and pop, and an overdrive in rock, but also in jazz for instance, distortion has no secrets for the experienced metal guitar player.

Two notes about the name distortion. It can be replaced by many other names to depict the same effect, but I have the impression that this name is both the most common and the most clear to everyone. Also, it is possible to say that a distortion is clean or not clean. This has nothing to do with the sound being less or more distorted, but with the distortion sound itself being sound or not sound. Indeed, many metal musicians spend a lot of time, research and money to obtaining the right gear and the right settings for the right distortion. Unfortunately, with a guitar for the beginner and an amp for the beginner, it is just not possible to make respected metal music. It would sound terribly. Paradoxically, beginners also tend to apply much more wet distortion than advanced metal players. Precisely because, when applied loosely, the distortion can end in chaos, the metal musician tends to "overcompensate" this, by almost obsessively controlling it in any way possible. He sometimes seems to spend more time to the set up, than to the actual playing. The neat result and the whole process, might appear even nerdy to some.

It is difficult to explain the distortion sound to someone with little knowledge about metal, or about audio waves in a technical way. Yet, it is not as complex as it may seem. Even though I prefer making promotion for promising obscure bands, it would probably be more efficient and effective again to refer to any song of "the good old Metallica" (in a legal way), and it should become clear what distortion is, when closely listening to the guitars, and comparing their sound with what is on the nearest radio. Especially because quite a lot of songs have acoustic effects as well, more often in the beginning of the songs, so the difference between the two would become clear at once. Also, it would become clear that leaving distortion aside for a moment, is also possible within metal music.

That distortion is more extreme than overdrive, does not mean however that the distortion sound would eventually result in more noise than the overdrive sound at all. Quite to the contrary, since playing with distortion requires a different and more controlling playing technique altogether. It would rather result in more noise, if the rock player were to use distortion instead of overdrive all of a sudden, maintaining his rock technique and theme. But, contrary to popular belief, also the basic rock sound itself might be more noisy, in a descriptive (not prescriptive) way. Let us just consider the hands of the right-handed guitar player. Concerning the left hand, the metal player is used to play what we could call an abbreviated form of a chord, having three consequences: it gets more powerful, as he even literally calls it a power chord, it gets less blurry, as there are simultaneously less different notes, and it gets more melodic, as there is more room to add individual notes after or before the chord has been struck.

This in combination with the right hand, definitely being no less important. A distinctive feature here is to prevent the notes or note to last as they would naturally do, by muting the strings with the right side of the palm. This is also practical because movements across the strings are mostly made with the wrist instead of the whole under-arm, as more frequent in other genres. This is only logical, since movements would be too many and too fast to do otherwise, and since relatively few strings are being hit at the same time in the first place. Another core feature of that hand, is to use a thick plectrum and to hold it farther away from the top of the index finger. While the former makes the sound more defined, the latter makes it possible to play faster. All put together, the consecutively muted hitting, mostly on lower frequencies on one string, intertwined with melodic themes, mostly on higher frequencies on more strings, would be an example of a system occuring quite a lot. Effectiveness and efficiency go literally hand in hand here. Effectiveness, because more melodies can be played, with a surplus of power. Efficiency, because once an advanced player of metal techniques, the result is obtained by the least possible complications and maximum control.

Some would bring in the notion of sustain to specify the metal guitars. It is true that the string being hit on a distorted guitar sounds significantly longer than the one on a guitar that is not distorted. Yet, the full potential of the sustain is seldom put into practice, because it would make things either too chaotic, or too slow. One could say that other instruments with sustain are the organ and the bagpipes. Yet, these are not considered part of the metal equipment as yet, rather of the church, or at least in it, and the clan. They have in common though the power that comes along with it. Also, it is very strange that people call metal loud music quite a lot. Of course, metal is just as loud as you put the volume, and it is a flaw of thinking that the music in itself would be loud or silent. Organs and bagpipes however, these are naturally quite loud, bereft of a simple volume button. Moreover, I have attended several concerts in very different genres, while getting suspicious looks with a sound level meter in my hand, and metal concerts proved to be not significantly louder.

Motörhead not included that is, the loudest band I have ever witnessed, but then the one and only Lemmy (the band's front man) assured us on stage that "we play rock & roll". While many metal heads worship him as the father, now grandfather, of metal, you never catch him pretending he is. He still seems to think in terms of rock or not, putting Metallica, The Ramones and The Beatles on the same line, what most metal heads actually would definitely not do. The Ramones would be considered punk, and as such too simple compared to metal, even though they share a certain nonconformist character. The Beatles would be considered mainstream pop-rock, even though they started experimenting with quite heavy overdrive at the time, symphonic arrangements and melomania. As pointed out earlier, even Metallica would not deserve the metal label of integrity according to quite a few, talking instead of "Moneytallica", or "Rocktallica" as Lars Ulrich himself (their drummer) suggested once. While many other bands would deserve a portion of their income, I would not agree with Lars, even though his obstinate ways are to be supported, because the overall way of guitar playing remains quite different, quite metal.

If we have to compare it to something, it would rather be like playing a violin that is down-tuned with six strings, frets, distortion and a hard plectrum. In this way, the most common underlying values of metal as music go hand in hand: technicality and power. Power without technicality could indeed result in punk for instance. Technicality without power could indeed result in the dominant interpretation of classical music for instance. Even though it is considered a keyboard instead of a string instrument like the violin and the guitar, the harpsichord would actually be the better comparison, for it has the sharp plucking and damper in common with metal guitar playing, enhancing precision, multitude and force. Of course, one can also play the electric guitar using metal guitar playing techniques without however using distortion at all. This logical possibility seems to be actualized by almost none though, other than Ice King again, and we would therefore hesitate to find this mechanism belonging to metal culture itself.

While a standard electric guitar begins with a low E string to a high E, metal guitars are often down-tuned, from D to D, or even from B to B. In the latter case, a seven string guitar is often being used to be able to still end with the high E, while keeping the regular tonal distances between the strings. Another extension is a guitar with more bars than usual. Combined with the compact shape of the metal guitar, its thin neck in particular, and its body cut out around the beginning of the neck, this means that virtuosity from very low to very high is very well being supported. Not only during solos, but also incorporated in the basic themes themselves, even though the distinction between the two may appear to be not that obvious in metal. The reason for this being that the notion of accompaniment is seldom at its place in metal music. Guitars, but also other instruments, are almost never just played as an accompaniment to something, but rather as a demanding purpose by itself, no less important than the vocals for instance.

Of course, bass guitars are also electric in metal music. Yet, distortion is not being used as often here. And if the effect is being used, it is in a less amount than with the (six string) guitars. The result is a more balanced, dynamic and even more powerful sound. The same amount is not principally out of the question, but mostly it just does not sound that good. While the bass guitar is traditionally being considered part of the rhythm section, this is not entirely true for metal. The explanation being that the bass guitar is, compared to other genres, much more being played as a guitar, than as a traditional bass guitar playing closely with the drums, and its lower kicks in particular - which are more scarce than in metal. This is not to say that the metal bass player does not pay attention to the drums, but that he would consider the traditional method somewhat too minimalistic. Also, this is not to say that all other genres play in a minimalistic way. Funk for instance is a very challenging genre for any bass player, and not that traditional, even though the playing technique is quite different from metal. Slapping and pulling does not occur often in metal, and many play with a plectrum instead of the fingers. Since bass guitars are far less compact than guitars, it is mostly not possible to play the same thing as on the guitar accurately, and it has more effect anyway to accentuate or elaborate particular parts of it instead. However, still a lot of notes are being played compared to other bass traditions.

Bass in general, whether it comes from the bass guitar, the low drums or the (muted) low guitar strings, is very important in metal to provide for the necessary punch. Yet, while it is somewhat mixed to the back on metal records, it often absorbs the other frequencies on live concerts. This is an inconsistency I would advise to resolve somehow. It seems like if you want to learn to imitate the guitar, you would better listen to the album, and if you want to learn to imitate the basses, you would better go to the concert, being less practical of course. Studio or stage though, metal bass players seem to not generally get as much attention as the other band members. Again, exceptions exist, and important ones, but you hardly ever get to see the name or photo of the bass player first in the booklet for instance, or his name with any of the composers or producers. Nor do you catch him standing in the middle or on the front row that much, nor does he get to play solos like the others, etcetera. Interviews are more common though, but then he usually seems to just have more time and enthusiasm for this than the others. Indeed, I would not say that the bass guitar is what most people think of as most prominent in metal music. Yet, if you were to leave it away, the sound would collapse like a house of cards sooner than you think.

4. Metal as music and more: voices

While instrumental metal bands exist, and while instrumental parts play a significant role within metal songs, the singer or vocalist remains the front man or woman. When outsiders tell, as they often do, that metal singers do nothing but yelling, they are wrong for three interrelated reasons. Firstly, if we were to assemble all metal vocals, about half of it would prove to be sung no less clean than in other genres. Moreover, there are more resemblances to opera singing in metal music than in any other genre. Secondly, the way someone yells who is getting into a fight on the street for instance, is technically and artistically entirely different from the way of "yelling" within metal music, otherwise the vocalist would have a sore throat all of the time, and would have to be kicked out of the band also because of lack of structured expression. Thirdly, the widest variety of "yelling", rough and clean singing exists within metal music, according to the widest variety of strict singing techniques and forms of expression. Many vocalists in the blues genre, in world music, rock, singer-songwriters etcetera, do sing with a rough voice. However, they never seem to get the critique that they are yelling too much. Quite unjust of course. Not that we have to start criticizing Louis Armstrong all of a sudden.

Not only is there a big difference in general singing styles between the abundant different sub genres within metal music. Also, it is possible to have many different singing styles within one metal song. If we made a parallel between the distortion effects on the guitars and the roughening of the vocals, there would be similarities but also differences. The disciplined way in which the musician picks and elaborates his particular distorted style would be the biggest similarity. It takes a lot of experience to grunt for instance the whole concert, and still give extensive interviews afterwards as if nothing happened. While it is true that not all who grunt for example are able to, or wish to, sing in the traditional way, it is definitely also true that not all who can sing in the traditional way know how to grunt. I myself find it more difficult in any case to sing with a grunting technique, than without it. Part of the reason is of course, and this counts as a difference, that generally no effects other than the human voice are being used in metal singing. Amplification, equalization, reverb and so forth are common, but, as we have pointed out, this does not as such affect the clarity of the natural voice. Consequently, we would better rephrase proper metal singing in terms of clean grunting for instance if it occurs, or clean falsetto if it occurs, which it does a lot, etcetera, instead of the possibly confusing clean or not clean singing as such.

What I told earlier, is to count as another difference: a distorted voice so to speak, is not being used in metal as often as a distorted guitar. In metal songs, much more, say, non-distorted vocals can be found than most people are willing to believe. Strangely enough, either these songs are less known by the popular audience, or these are known even though the popular audience does not realize it is metal. It is almost never right to have a one-sided opinion about something, and definitely not about metal nor its music, and "the" metal vocals should be one of the clearest examples why. Because quite all of the extremities of singing can be found in metal music alone, not only from extremely rough to extremely angelic, but also from extremely low to extremely high, from extremely rhythmical to extremely melodic, from extremely fast to extremely slow, from extremely extroverted to extremely introverted, from extremely negative to extremely positive, and on and on. If one wants to be opposed to metal, one-sidedness can never correctly be the cause. Call it expressionism, that could be a correct cause indeed. But then, why would one want to be opposed to expressiveness?

Another face of (vocal) expressiveness in metal is the serious concern, more than average, about phonetics. When it comes down to it, the musical aspect of the text, or lyrics as it is being called, is generally even more important than the dictionary meaning of the words. This is not to say that the words should be articulated precisely in the way the dictionary prescribes. To the contrary, the words should be articulated precisely in the way the metal song, and what it is to express, prescribes. Words are being chewed, stretched, scanned, re-accentuated or, if "vowel" was a verb, re-vowelled. At the end of many a metal chorus for instance, sustain of the vocals, quite literally displaying the content of the lungs of the singer, could resemble to the sustain on the guitars as discussed earlier. However, the guitars would have started with the new verse already, while the vocals make the bridge. The active treatment of the vocal sounds could be called revolutionary: while traditionally the way of singing rather adapts itself to the lyrics, the latter thereby stealing the show, in metal the lyrics are rather adapted to the way of singing and expressing. When metal songs are being "written", the actual lyrics are often the very last thing (and in fact the only thing literally) being written, after the vocal lines have already been set out. This shows that vocals can be treated as instruments, and that sounds can have a rich meaning, not necessarily having anything to do with their conventional non-musical content *a posteriori*.

However, this does not mean at all that lyrics are not being considered important in metal. Otherwise there would not even be lyrics, but just vocal sounds. It rather means that so much music can be found in metal vocals, that it is perfectly possible to value it for a lifetime without any reference to the lyrics. This is also a point where a distinction between metal and metal as music could enter the discussion. If you are above all a fan of metal as music, it is quite realistic that you can sing along with the song, without extrapolating or even realizing its lyrical content. If you are above all a metal head vis-à-vis the world, it is quite realistic that you take the lyrics into consideration, incorporate them somehow in your world view or lifestyle, and take the music itself sideways in its psycho-social meaning. Again, this is a theoretical bifurcation overlapping more or less in practice.

There are many outsiders who are keen on underlining the negative consequences of metal lyrics, in their language metal (as such), and the lack of musical qualities of metal music, in their language metal (as such). *Sed contra*: not only has a causal relation between metal lyrics and vaguely put negative consequences never been proven, but also and consequently is the hypothesis equally valid that the music itself, with or without the lyrics even, has positive consequences, and not only is the content of metal lyrics only one cluster of pieces amongst many different others within the metal puzzle, but also and consequently shows actual analysis of the inherently musical clusters the many different qualities of metal as music rather than the lack of them.

As expressive and extreme the metal vocals, as expressive and extreme the metal lyrics. The lyrics of the song being played in the supermarket seem to be eager to confirm hollow romances, material things and worldly dos and don'ts. Upon hearing this, two reactions are possible. Either, and this seems to be mostly the case, otherwise marketeers would not have it played anymore, you take it in as a welcome distraction from both outer and inner silence, thereby silencing any subsequent questioning, and as a comforting re-affirmation of current societal norms, making them seem natural, easy and settled. Or you think: if I was to write lyrics in a way that confronts us least with any fundamental issues, I would write lyrics like these. I am not implying that metal heads have a monopoly of the latter reaction, or that this is their explicit reaction instead of their intuitive reaction. I am quite sure that metal-hating philosophers for instance think likewise, if they ever enter a supermarket themselves at all.

Indeed, the first 101 topics that come to my mind when I think of metal lyrics, are: death, life, light, night, dark, cold, north, winter, fire, desire, sex, love, hate, killing, anger, fear, war, apocalypse, nuclear, terror, horror, destruction, deformation, depression, megalomania, power, consciousness, will, fate, faith, religion, gods, demons, angels, ghosts, occultism, heathenism, heroic, honour, hope, courage, victory, failure, loss, tragedy, comedy, surreality, abstract, insanity, pain, blood, ugliness, beauty, beastly, evil, justice, truth, lies, masses, chaos, anarchic, totalitarian, politics, corruption, order, nature, cosmos, future, history, nostalgia, mystery, fantasy, sagas, legends, knights, kings, vikings, vampires, pirates, rebellion, slavery, machines, misanthropy, alienation, addiction, alcohol, partying, head banging, togetherness, solitude, wildness, touring, loudness, motors, steel, speed, eagles, freedom, independence, authenticity and metal itself.

Of course, this list is only indicative, not exhaustive. While you are invited to discover other themes, chances are high that they also have got something to do with, in brief, "high" or "low". It seems that metal wants to avoid anything that is average, in favour of both heights and depths. Nothing is OK. It is either superb, or terrible, possibly at the same time and place. This, in contrast with societal expectations. Society implicitly demands us to ask to people pretty constantly "everything OK?", and to respond with "everything OK!", or variations on the same theme. If we do not do this, many people get surprised and even shocked. Yet, if we are honest with ourselves and with the others, it is hard to find even one person on this Earth with whom literally everything is really OK. And if we found one, it would probably go hand in hand with the not everything being OK for someone else. At a particular time and place, certain parts of certain things are better than just OK, and certain, and perhaps most, parts of things are actually worse. Far more struggles both inside and among people are going on than they usually allow themselves to admit. This is only human. The image and expectation of man as promoted by most advertisements, recruitment managers, mediocre motion pictures and waiting music for instance, that is not very human. They are inclined to portray a man having but one thin and faint dimension, getting supposedly well-earned fortune, not questioning, not being on a perpetual quest, in short: a man not being at all.

It is a merit of metal I think to not pretend all is alright always and everywhere. The ways of expressing this, are diverse and sometimes even contradictory though. Some describe situations, thoughts or feelings just as they appear to be, while others prescribe how they ought to be, and still others describe them as they are not, by just escaping to other times or places, while some transcribe them to elaborate the strength within, by overcompensating as it were. Another merit would be to find beauty and truth were most do not find it, encompassing a big source of misunderstandings. When an outsider is criticizing all the negativism associated with metal, perhaps he is actually criticizing himself after all. From the earliest stage in life, people are easily surrounded by colours, light, warmth, seeming simplicity, talking animals, talking as such, adults acting more friendly than usual and more childish than the child himself, etcetera. As if there cannot be value in the big gray scale, the dark, the cold, complex subtlety, nature as it is, silence, as if adults are always innocent givers who need to act in a familiar and unreflected way, etcetera. Of course, if one cannot find any beauty or truth in the dark, both literally and figuratively, one sees metal as negative. But, in doing so, he is rather displaying his own negativity that he projects, than the negativity in metal or anything else itself.

In addition to this, it is to be noted that relatively many metal fans spontaneously declare themselves fan of the philosopher, but also philologist, poet and composer Nietzsche, Friedrich. Many times have I tested how well they know what he actually wrote. Almost as many times have I been disappointed though. The vast majority had obviously not read anything more yet than a few translated quotes on the web, résumés of secondary writings or the back flap of the book on their shelve. I seemed to have read more, as demanded by my past philosophy courses, while I do not even consider myself to be a real fan of him. As it often occurs in history, something or someone becomes a brand representing something not necessarily representing the original. This also seems to be the case with Nietzsche as worshipped by metal, but also gothic, enthusiasts. Ironically, as with metal itself: the more you know about a phenomenon like Nietzsche and his academic followers, the less you think you can make a, by now traditional, powerpoint presentation of ten minutes so to speak, supposed to making the matter truthfully clear. Metal is a complex matter. Nietzsche is a complex matter. Metal fans dwelling with Nietzsche without knowing too much about him, should think of people dwelling with metal without knowing too much about it.

Thus, more compelling in this book at least, is the question what Nietzsche as a brand represents in metal. Quite coincidentally, the name Nietzsche itself already uncovers the clue. In the Germanic linguistic tradition, "niet-" means the absence or counterpart of something, thereby becoming respectively "not some thing" (nothing) or "not that thing" (something other). Either way, it is not the affirmation of the present as posed: positivity. It is in this sense negativity, and this is precisely what many metal fans seem to be attracted to. This could be because they do not favour authority, or because they do not favour the immanent. Stating positivity is more conventional than the opposite, and so one could experience it as an authoritative claim, pushing the individual in a certain direction, and by doing so, threatening his modern ideal or even right to think and act autonomously. Stating positivity also poses what is immanent in a thing, setting or thought, instead of what transcends it. In this way too, the modern individual could find the mechanism choking, preferring or even needing on the contrary what goes beyond normal limits or boundaries, because it is deemed more significant than them: transcendence.

Who hears the word transcendence, could associate it with God. Yet, also God is by most metal heads associated with the pressing affirmation of the mainstream, and even cover-up for mischievous practices. Theoretically, I see no reason why it would not be possible to elaborate another transcendent system. Practically however, metal heads do not as a rule seem to try to endeavour this, and just counter-attack the positivity/promote the vague negativity as such. In this way, they have something important in common with the reactionary attacker of metal though: they do their best to maintain a dualism, to be recognized as being part of a group that eventually says yes to societal norms or no. The turning point being that the subscription to the positive values, or "to the contrary" the counterpart values, is perceived as being more important than the exploration of reasons for a particular value in a particular case. The latter perspective not defending monism or pluralism as a rule, but just not pretending things are as simple as dualism. So, Nietzsche may have become associated with the umbrella of defending the opposite, yet personal analysis shows that this kind of opposite is not really an opposite, and that playing either the bourgeois, or the teenager who resents him, should not be the only option. If both were in a strong position, which they nonetheless claim, they would not put so much effort in defending themselves towards the other in the first place, and look inwards and onwards instead. Yes, metal deals with fundamental topics, which is more than we can say of many other genres. No, it does not, or not yet, use its full theoretical, critical and self-critical potential.

Any practices based upon incomplete theories are thereby also incomplete and ineffective. As pointed out earlier, no matter how extreme and even devilish metal lyrics may be, there is no sound proof of a causal relation between them and extreme, angelic or devilish behaviour. There are multiple signs though of metal music being able to calm people down, who would otherwise perhaps tend to get involved into such behaviour. But what does this change? After the metal head has calmed down, certain matters of fact which he finds displeasing, remain exactly what they were. And for sure, he will get winded up again sooner or later. If metal lyrics were just one part of a broad metal discourse questioning particular problems and working out particular solutions and particular ways to implement them, the resenting metal head could perhaps listen to his favourite music one day for the love of music instead of the need to have some calming down effect, with the risk of perverting the music as functional music. Yet, there are not many signs of making such a way out, and if there were: I did not say that day is likely to come very soon.

With functional music, I mean the music not being the end in itself, but the music being a means or function towards some other end. These functions can be multiple, and hybrid forms containing both musically essential and different functional aspects are mostly the case in practice in a higher or lower degree. Politics for instance, seems to generally assume a functional interpretation of music. The quality of music is measured against the quantity of what is called participation for instance, say passive receivers or jobs like any other, against the success of the non-musical cause where the music is playing, the payoff of the investment etcetera, rarely against musical qualities as such. An idea worth examining in another treatise. On the contrary, one might think that professional musicians support a less functional/more "essentialist" view on music. Yet, this is a tricky thought. Precisely because music for the professional musician has also the function of providing for an income, the non-professional musician is in fact more likely to develop an essentialist style. Of course, I mean "professional" in an economic way, not in the sense that it would by definition encompass music that is essentially more rich than that of the talented and experienced "amateur".

To try to show by the means of certain music that one is at odds with society as a whole or personal circumstances, could also be considered a function. The position of many enough metal heads is problematic here. Many indeed seem to claim that metal is the only true way of revolting, which does not make things less ambivalent. Not only could the same signal be given using different music, also could the same music be used giving another signal. In theory, but also in practice. If we were to encounter the inventors of what we have come to call metal, back then, we would sooner think that they are hippies than that they are metal heads - the profile being exploited only much later. Now however, a die hard metal head does not wish to be looked at as a hippie. The association with colours, sunshine, love, peace, and perhaps even chaos, it does not particularly fit in his image of the warrior say. Or let us consider the blues. While the lyrics in blues are not significantly less rebellious and even devilish than in metal, and while early metal is musically quite strongly interrelated with the blues genre, you almost never get to see metal heads mixed up with the blues community now, and even more strikingly, as a matter of fact rather than politics, black people as such - not at the least in reverse.

As a consequence, one might wonder what was first: the music or its function? Music only exists by being made by particular people or being received by particular people. Speaking in general terms would make us believe either that all people think the same, or that music has an existence in the same way people exist. Regardless whether people themselves have a function or not, you can say that something is first to them or not though, for instance a monkey. When people use the word metal, some actually mean the music, others actually mean its function, and still others actually mean both, however in the most varying proportions. Sound qualities as such are not able to speak for themselves as having this or that function, or none at all. Interpretations of a particular person of those sound qualities on the other hand, are. When the lyrics come into play, more things than sound qualities are involved: the content of the words. It does not come as a surprise then that many misunderstandings are also being developed by using the word music, by the one meaning the mere sounds qualities as such, by the other also the lyrical references, the way those sound qualities are being framed, used or misused, etcetera.

More generally, the question can be asked what should

prevail: the art or the good? Someone like Plato would answer the good. Someone like Nietzsche would answer the art, not that metal fans seem to be aware of this element. Someone like me would find the question not very clear. Firstly, it is not clear what the art and the good are lining up for. If they are standing in the same row, we could say something like "first come, first served" if the issue is not clear. If the issue is clear, then we cannot answer without knowing it. And if there are different rows for different accounts, they require another sort of answer and question. It would be absurd to say that a man standing in the row at the bank office should be served sooner than the man in the row at the post office. Secondly, the question itself what should prevail is a question of an ethical sort (concerning the good/bad). Thus, by responding alone, the art would come last. And it often comes last, even when people pretend that it comes first. The first minute they want to talk about the meaning of art, the next minutes they start talking about its utilities. The meaning does not care about its utility though, and if it would, the meaning would vanish soon enough. To be sure, this is not to be confused with utilitarianism. Simply put, this -ism states that the goodness of something depends on (the advantages of) the consequences of it. Instead of focusing on the goodness of something in itself or its good intentions. Yet, also defenders of the latter category, once outside the field of ethics and entering the field of aesthetics, seem to be more concerned with the (non utilitarian) ethical consequences of aesthetics than with aesthetics in itself. In this respect, one might wonder why philosophers like Plato should have become so popular.

Side B - A matter of time

5. Apollo, Dionysus and other gods

While relatively many metal heads assume support for their attraction to "the opposite" by loosely referring to Nietzsche, it is an as yet missed opportunity that they overlook still another theme in the writings of Nietzsche which is of no less importance in trying to clarify metal as being played, as being sung and as being spoken of: Apollo and Dionysus. Nietzsche did not invent this theme though. It has been a core topic both in ancient Greek mythology itself, and the rich literary tradition about it that followed. Also because of the latter, it is strange that the subject did not get too much attention yet: because metal lyrics are otherwise quite classical, in the sense that references - true or false - to mythology and historical names and plots are abundant without overstatement.

Dionysus and Apollo are sons of the god Zeus. Dionysus is being associated with chaos, emotion, instinct, ecstasy, intoxication, wine, submission, the whole, sensuality, unjust, fate, pleasure, experience, ostentatiousness, excess, darkness, femininity, wildness, nature, destruction,... Apollo is being associated with reason, control, power, masculinity, light, structure, clarity, solidity, orientation, progress, harmony, order, virtue, restraint, modesty, ideas, individuality, civilization, health, discipline,... While in the meantime, many tend to associate music rather with Dionysus, it is clear that for the ancient Greeks the Apollo "type" was the better musician and poet, and even the better human being as such. In the same way, Dionysus was more associated with wind instruments and percussion, and Apollo with the back then higher estimated string instruments and vocal parts. It is not our concern here who is the best, if any of the two is to be. It is our concern though that general perception of metal goes implicitly into the direction of Dionysus, while there are definitely no less Apollonian elements. An exception seems to exist though, where metal is explicitly being associated with Dionysus in an elaborate way. By Deena Weinstein that is, in her book "Heavy Metal, The Music and Its Culture" (rev. ed. 2000, first ed. 1991). Even though it is one of the most respected books in the (very small) field, her exclusively

Dionysian interpretation distorts to quite an extent the main features of metal culture, obscures the diversity of the people nourishing that culture and the inner ambivalence of even one person therein.

While the impulse of putting a metal band together, record your own metal songs and go touring, may emerge late at night in a flashy bar with your pals having wine, in this case probably beer, the actual doing of it the next morning demands a great effort of Apollonian thinking and doing. Fans of metal start indeed playing the music themselves relatively more than in other genres. Overview of the local bands and adverts of musicians seeking other musicians, of releases analogue or digital, and running order of non-subsidized (yet not for profit) concerts, shows that metal is represented more on this active level than its overall representation on the passive, say Dionysian, level of mere fans of this or that genre would suggest. The image of "sex, drugs, and rock & roll" would suggest the life of a Dionysus though. While this image building paradoxically appears to be a successful marketing strategy for the disguised Apollo, metal musicians who can even afford to keep both the Dionysian lifestyle and their music, are far more exception than rule. As we have already uncovered, the tremendous amount of practice needed, alone and with a selected disciplined band, the composing itself, the research and managing of recording, releasing, opportunities to play and media, the promoting, the investment of money, time, space even and social sacrifices,... not really Dionysus' cup of tea of course. And if metal is the religion of hedonism, as Weinstein wants to show, then why is it so serious about anything dark, bitter and epic in this world, instead of sea, sun and fun? The latter would be the core business of Club Med, not Club Metal.

In public perception though, it seems that artists as such are being associated with Dionysus. During a recruitment interview, I have even been asked once: "how come you give (musical) shows and such, and yet lack the spontaneity that we seek?". My reply: "for two obvious reasons. Firstly, if I were as spontaneous as you are dreaming of, I would not be able to organize, plan and execute a qualitative show, and even if I would, I would not have composed, practiced and directed anything qualitative enough to show in the first place. Secondly, if I were as spontaneous, I would not be applying for this job, nor any other place I would expect to work at, but apparently my expectations do not fit reality in this case." Back to our case. The Dionysian perception of art is being promoted by both political and societal structures, doing their best to "functionalise" art as mere means to distraction, socialization, socializing and *la dépense*. This, in sharp contrast with artists who consider it their primary device and even vocation: concentration both from the sender of the art and the receiver, artistic liberty regardless of its critical potency or condition, and literal or figurative communication as far away as possible from small talk, keeping up appearances and cheap and soulless consumerism. The consequence quite often being that, for the sake of making a living, either the "artist" compromises, or the artist gets another job and works in her spare time for her own art. Not much Dionysus for the latter.

I just used the word "her", but in most cases it is still a "he" indeed who makes the music, manages it, organizes events, puts together a collection, maintains websites, in fact being industrious on all metal fronts. At concerts and other dress up gatherings more and more females are attending though. In relatively a lot of cases they just come along with their boyfriend who happens to be a metal head. I have known a lot of girls stopping to give interest to the music, not only at shows but especially at the record shop, as soon as a boyfriend switch came up. But of course women exist who are really interested in it, as men exist who just walk along with anything that appears to be socially convenient at the time and place. A particular mechanism is at work though concerning femininity in metal. Bluntly put, it seems that either the woman "has to" adapt to the male way, or "has to" become an object for lust. Integrating feminine ways without ending up in the latter category, is as yet surprisingly and disappointingly rare.

So, while it is true that the metal fan is no longer highly exceptionally a woman, the male model quite prevails. Women often dress up like the men have been doing, and copy their behaviour. In this way they are being respected as much as any fellow metal man, in the way a disguised woman would be if she came along to the battlefield say, not just to fetch the water but to fight. Most woman concerned with the metal music, I am not taking about gothic music for instance or metal groupies, seem to take this path indeed, to enter the realm of (manly) brotherhood, which seems to be quite different from sisterhood. Who has witnessed the change in schools for instance from all male or all female to mixed, easily gets the gist. Regardless any side-effects, the male class being united against the establishment as it were, entertains an remarkable bond of boyish behaviour, a playful solidarity of the kind of partners-in-crime. The feeling of "we", lost on many other accounts of modern Western society, comes in through the back door, strong but fragile when dispersed by, in this case female, exogenous input. Since the sex topic is seldom elaborated in its subtle or cultivated forms in metal, perhaps also a consequence of the tradition of adolescent males having been the protagonists, the option of a lust object is also valid, dressing up then in the other extreme. The practice of groupies for instance being accepted. Yet, too many of them, would compete with the masculine dominance and the still taking very serious of the metal music. While the aforementioned professor Weinstein maintains a corresponding analysis of masculinity in metal, she - knowingly or not - forgets to mention that masculinity is typically associated with Apollo, not Dionysus. But then she never writes (about) Apollo, perchance because the professor is not male after all.

That the act itself of creating metal music has much more to do with Apollo than many who do not or cannot do it themselves, does not mean that the musical content resulting cannot encompass Dionysian elements. Considering the instrumental content, it is often the result and the purpose to bring wildness and darkness to life. At the same time, the music often wants to exhibit control and power. Actually, there is no contradiction here. It is precisely because wildness is being brought to life in such a controlled way, that it is so effective. Also with regard to this, parallels with the mechanism of war come to the forefront. Yes, display of war creates the convincing effect of destruction. Yet, this is being done not in spite of, but precisely "thanks to" an abundance of military intelligence and obsession with order. Moreover, acts of war are almost never being carried out for the mere appetite for chaos. Instead for a new order, in the light of which the current order is being considered chaotic.

There exists a wide variety of so-called sub genres within, overlapping with or relating to metal though, and this affects many variables in the metal research, including the Dionysus-Apollo balance. Considering the most established sub genres, as put on the map later, we might already point out that power metal entails an awful lot of Apollonian elements and doom metal relatively a lot of Dionysian elements. It is no surprise then that fans of both sub genres at the same time seem to be rather scarce, and that the latter has relatively a lot of success with women. But even if I say Dionysian elements, this is not Dionysus himself. He would rather lay back and improvise of course, well or not well, than concentrate on strictly executing a strongly structured, even (not formulaic, but) "formulistic" metal song, the technical perfection and order of which is to sustain the almost mythical character of the song as a thing in itself (reification) and larger than life. Especially larger than the plain daily life from which Dionysus would be a mere nightly escape, while the Apollonian song is to represent an alternative world on an alternative level, keeping up the spirit night and day alike. Improvisation is far from common in metal. A guitar soloist may improvise sometimes, but the audience seems to prefer otherwise, saying to their neighbour that the studio solo must have been to difficult to replay without the risk of (what is seen as) failure.

This is probably the biggest difference with jazz for instance, even with progressive metal bands, not the complexity of the music, not the technicality, not the so-called loudness, but the intended indeterminacy in jazz versus the static model in metal. Also, improvisation, the unique event where composition and execution are the very same process, would make the music seem relative: it could have been different. This idea however does not suit the main metal course. Songs, albums, whole bands even, are to be absolute as it were. Perhaps because in the eyes of the metal head, the rest of the world seems to lack absoluteness. Significant changes, musical style, visual artwork or any other, may be appreciated by the fans after a while, but feared at first and mostly criticized ever after. It is not like: let us have a party tonight and everyone who happens to be there plays an instrument. No, a band member being replaced is given almost the attention the way we would when finding out that one of the twelve apostles was actually another one.

The visuals themselves are almost always highly Apollonian also. A mere glance at the metal band logos, omnipresent in the metal club, should immediately give away the utmost attention to the elaborate, symmetric, geometric, integrative, calligraphic, polished, static and homogenous in style in time and place. The passion for something "finished", in other words: perfectionism, extends itself to all derivative products as well. Sometimes the logo is not even legible anymore by metal tourists, which is not to say recognizable, because the value of a work of art (artwork) prevails. Something written or drawn in the frame of metal is never an inadvertent sketch, it is never "just". It is deliberate, and rarely even deliberately appearing impulsive. This they have in common with the medieval monks actually, more being artists than copyists, worshipping - at least in doing so - another than Dionysian god. Paradoxically, the "artwork" accompanying old music nowadays, has at times more in common with the layout of transport time tables, than with anything cultivated. This also shows why Apollo is unjustly being associated with Spartan, the latter putting all his energy to keeping things as simple as possible, void of imagination.

Considering the lyrical content, putting together our previous series of words appearing in metal lyrics and in the Dionysian and Apollonian repertoire, shows that neither of the types has a monopoly. Again, putting yourself to writing the lyrics itself is a demanding job in the vein of Apollo. Not only do the lyrics themselves have to express some kind of coherent meaning, other than "I luv u babe" so to speak, they also have to correspond somehow to the expression, and I mean expression, of the vocal sounds alone, and there is quite a tension between the two, awaiting the attention of the metal writer, the approval of his demanding band mates and his utmost demanding fans alike. In metal also, concept albums and stories even crossing multiple albums are no exception. The easiest way out is seldom being taken.

To talk about a certain theme though, does not mean that that theme is being practiced by the one who does the talking. Very simple, but very important and often forgotten. To talk about the unjust, does not mean that there is less justice in the world by doing so. To talk about power, does not mean that there is more power all of a sudden, and so forth. So, to talk about a Dionysus or an Apollo, or even the need to represent their world, does not mean to be one of them. If it is to mean something, several other explications are possible. It can mean that it is being considered interesting, and as such worthy of telling, regardless what is right or wrong. Like metal lyricists, poets or academics can write about excess. Yet, to expect the lyricist to be more excessive than the others, is just unjust. Metal lyricists also talk more than other lyricists about mythical, historical and historic themes. Yet, to expect them to be more well-read than the academic, is just unjust. If it is to mean something functional, one could say that the extreme styles help to frame and understand an otherwise chaotic world. It has this in common with myths also. Monkeys do not invent myths, because they do not care to make sense of the world. People do, and those who take it to an extreme we call philosophers. While myths were created in a pre-technological or artisan era though, one could argue that the current "over-technologization" creates a new sort of chaos, evoking mythical, historical and artistic reflexes being pushed away in daily life.

Another functional meaning could be that both appetites and fears are being resolved by the cathartic effect of merely expressing them. This could be for instance, the quadrant: an appetite for destruction (no reference meant to the album of Guns N' Roses), an appetite for order, a fear for destruction, a fear for order. Any example here is more complex than it might appear though. While appetites for destruction might remind some of Dionysus, this has conceptually nothing to do with him. To have an appetite for destruction, or to have an appetite for wine, as such does not mean to destruct or to drink. I would say even more: to have such appetites, and yet not execute them, is being accompanied by much more Apollonian discipline than to not have the appetites in the first place. Merely thinking or dreaming something can never be immoral, only the decision to put it into practice.

A possible misunderstanding is also that the popular theme of destruction should have an immoral flavour. One of the reasons however that it keeps on being a popular theme, is that it is being considered shocking. A similar mechanism is at work then with the child that plays with something that is forbidden, just because it is forbidden, and it does not really matter what that is precisely. Someone truly immoral is not that much concerned with being shocked, someone else being shocked or being recognized as someone shocking though, than with just getting the immoral thing done. Also, one would expect that for someone constantly exposed to a theme like destruction, it would not be a big thing anymore. The undertaker can pretend he is profoundly moved each time someone dies a natural death, yet after thousands and thousands of cases (figuratively and literally), there is a kind of callus on the soul. Yet, the metal head seems to be passionate each time and again the word death alone sees daylight, which happens literally all the time there. This is a token that the metal head is rather a hyper-sensitive than someone not caring, often too easily associated with the terms nihilism and cynicism.

A resuming complexity is the quite likely possibility to have an appetite for destruction and order, and to fear order and destruction all at the very same time, without being contradictory. Namely, if what we have been taught to call order is being uncovered as disorder and destruction of an absent appealing order that can be attained by destructing the current "order". Whoever criticizes the status quo, has three entirely different options, which could however occur at the same time also. Firstly, to expose the wrong side of it. Secondly, to indicate what and how it is to change. Thirdly, to expose the alternative order. Metal lyrics, graphics and what we might call beginnings of discourses, are mostly concerned with the first option, sometimes with the third, and rarely with the second. If someone would do the opposite of the first: expose all the positive sides of the establishment and negate the negative ones, we would think the person is either naive to be blind for injustice and inhumanity, or harsh to legitimize his own luck at the expense of other human and other beings, either fatalistic to not think mankind could do otherwise, or a coward to just not want to get into trouble. In this sense, metal is seldom naive, harsh, fatalistic or cowardly. Nuclear threats, partial judges, holy wars,.... the list is so long that not one single malpractice seems to be out of sight of the metal head. By displaying so, the conceptual, and sometimes very concrete, wrongdoers are getting the symbolic punishment they are not expected to get in daily life.

If we praise probably correctly, after having read his remarkable Personal Memoirs, General Ulysses S. Grant for instance for having succeeded to end the American Civil War in the 19th century, by carrying it out in quite the most reasonable way possible regarding the circumstances, and thereby end official slavery, most of us now do not hold back. In his own words: "although a soldier by profession, I have never felt any sort of fondness for war, and I have never advocated it, except as a means of peace". Yet, if the cover of a metal album displays men in suits having chained the people, say still existing non-official slavery, and the back of the album displays those men being torn apart by some kind of moral monster, the difference is not as big as many want to believe.

There is a difference however, but another one. While someone like Grant is concerned and capable considering our option two: what and how to do for the better, metal does not offer any perspectives most of the time. Sometimes a metal utopia is being constructed, yet the making of the bridge towards it remains either obliterated, or utopian itself. One could of course argue that generals or politicians are paid for or empowered to resolving societal issues, whereas metal heads are neither. The metal artist himself is generally not even reimbursed and recognized adequately with regard to his art, so it is difficult to see how he could elaborate the activism and motivation as yet another gift in the spare time he cannot even afford to have. More fundamentally, metal heads display a lot of resentment, resulting in some moral mathematics: "if society does not care about us, then why should we care about society?". What is easily interpreted by outsiders as an immoral threat to society, and what is easily used by insiders for recognition as a rebel, is instead a plain moral concern then: fairness.

Even more fundamentally, any activism would immediately attack the metal fortress from within. It would become clear that few people share the same ideas once it is not about vague ideas anymore. For instance, no one is against freedom, so often promoted in metal, yet any philosopher knows that when it comes down to it, the term is being interpreted in a multitude of often contradictory ways, and is challenging other values which are being promoted at the same time, for instance the idea of a (worldwide) metal nation. Also, it would become clear that metal is not constructed in some sort of a vacuum in society, which simply cannot exist, and that society depends on both the daily contributions of the metal heads as workers or consumers, and on metal's "container revolution", which would become a problem if the revolutionaries would take it outside the container or fortress.

Paradoxically, we can even suspect that metal is a new form of opium of/for the people, to an air of Karl Marx. While most metal heads would be the first ones to approve the crushing down of any power of any religion, they do not seem to fear that metal too could easily have the "advantage" of keeping the people, or some at least, calm. They do not seem to fear that the ritualistic experience of a metal show could be a clever substitute for the Mass. Thereby giving the people something to believe in when they experience things they do not believe in after and before it, and resolving the tensions in daily life by releasing them in the church/venue, after which the next week can begin without too much societal disturbance.

To an air of Nietzsche then, it is considered "cool" among metal heads to say that god is dead, whether or not their knowledge of Nietzsche is sufficiently adequate. If this would be said by some *Einzelgänger*, not willing to get involved in any common worship and ritualistic behaviour, not interested in transgressing the daily material and materialistic world, and not adhering to any background system giving both meaning and comfort to his short existence, we might consider believing him. Yet, in their active reluctance to religion, metal heads tend to treat metal as if it were some religion indeed. As if metal were a union, internally harmonious and clearly distinct from any external elements, as if the unwritten rules about metal were a Bible to be followed, instead of questioned and elaborated, as if the falling apart of the religious social network needed to be replaced by another one, in this case the metal community, as if membership of this community were for a lifetime and even "deathtime" or not at all, as if metal membership were not to be cumulated with any "concurring" memberships, as if there should be hanging a cross, turned upside down or not, or other symbol again in the room or around the neck, as if going to a metal festival far away were a pilgrimage, the sacrifices of which proving your belief, as if anything acquired there should be displayed as a relic of belonging, well conduct and stimulus to do even better on the ladder to metal heaven, as if the festival itself were not just the coming together of a bunch of people with some overlapping musical tastes, but also the gathering of the select ones who found the right path and the reconstitution itself of their sacred bond, as if merely executing the songs and consequently clapping hands were not enough, and community serving rituals need to be carried out before, during, and after the songs, as if playing the best known songs over and over again each festival were a welcome way of creating anthems to be sung together and affirming the overall linkage in time and place, as if the iconography, sequence and preaching on stage and your spot, Sunday clothes and cooperation in the audience were to reflect a larger than life system, as if drinking any fluid were not just a comforting relief or prevention of personal thirst, but the drinking of beer together is to be stressed in the way of a Communion, etcetera.

Etymologically, religion is to re-legio or re-ligare, which is to re-assemble meanings or re-assemble people. In a certain sense - a sociological one, not a theological one - this is what metal does, if not by purpose, then by consequence. That there is no Bible or Catechism, does not mean though that there is the rule of chaos as many want to believe. To the contrary, the unwritten rules have become so strict that it is easier even to recognize a fellow metal head than a fellow Christian. This produces a sincere problem: at the one hand metal is supposed to be an expression of liberty exempt from "the system", at the other hand it maintains a system of its own in which social conventions are taken very seriously. The mainstream ideas within the metal group about the sounding, the appearing and the behaving, are much more followed than put to question. It might seem comic, but actually it is very significant, one of many similar occasions on which I happened to tell to a fellow metal fan, with a cup of tea in my hand and wearing a white shirt, that I had been listening to the albums Load and Re-load of Metallica a lot lately, that I would leave the event we were at to do some further writing of a paper and made an early appointment with the hairdresser the next day. He asked back: "what is the matter with you?".

If I did not want to get into an awkward position, all I had to do was to wear a black shirt, have a beer, hang around, drop the name Moneytallica once in a while and let my hair annoy me. One might wonder how much rebellion there really is though, when risky colours are not being worn, when social drinking is to be respected as social, when critical thought is sooner brought to life at a silent desk than at a loud meeting, when outer appearance is more important than practicality and what is inside the head, and when the community decides in your place which albums you ought to like. For the record, if Metallica was above all interested in money, they would just have all their previous albums remixed and remastered, extended with a few bonus tracks and extra artwork in multiple fancy editions, which they still have not. They could easily have put, a strategy taken by so many others, a "Master of Puppets - Part II" album on the market (the original album released in 1986 and worshipped by fans and encyclopedia writers alike), yet their own stubbornness is clearly more dear to them than the pleasing of the average fan. This attitude is an artistic one, not an economic one, and shared with many other metal bands. The main difference being that the band was so extremely lucky to be at the right time on the right spot, and that they can do whatever they want without endangering their pension. Concerning the aspect of being heavy, Metallica's first album, which one is "allowed to" like in the metal community, might have been heavier than most other music around at the time (early eighties) unlike Load and Re-Load (later nineties), yet close listening and comparing of all of these records, which is seldom being done, proves that the debut, as being played back then, is actually lighter to swallow than the later couple. Having convinced the few customers of my shop who took the time to partake in the experiment, I regard as one of my most important memoirs. It means not only that social perceptions are often more real than actual perceptions, but also that these can be adjusted to actuality under the right circumstances and discipline.

Even though autonomy is valued highly in metal, also metal heads can be prone to the social system. When I was selling albums, selling rates proved what I found counter-intuitive: the more an album had been sold, the bigger the chance that it would be sold even more. Also: the more a ticket had been sold, the bigger the chance that it would be sold even more, etcetera. If this mechanism was fed by the personal need for a qualitative product, it could not explain why many equally and more qualitative products did not get sold. Therefore, it is more plausible that the "personal" need is being fed, not decisively by intrinsic criteria concerning the product, but by the social acceptance itself. Relatively many do not want to miss out on "what is happening". It gives them the feeling of being part of something big, something to believe in, barely examining anymore what the thing actually is or which other things deserve to be big and believed in. Thereby creating the contradiction of course when metal heads claim to step back from social conformity by just creating another form of social conformity.

This is not particularly different from other genres. A pop artist does not appear on TV because his music is outstanding, but because he appears on TV his music is deemed outstanding. One might even extend it outside the musical field: something becomes the news because it gets on the news and how it gets on the news. More and more even the news is referring to other programs or websites as a source of news, thereby remaining within the level of media, weakening the reference to any actual happening. The similarities with Plato's cave are striking. In a few - too few - words: daily life is being compared by him to a cave, where people only see the shadows of outer reality instead of reality itself, not realizing that they are only shadows. One can only escape from the realm of shadows by examining - in a dialectical way - what a thing is in itself, exempt from extrinsic criteria. This is both a lonely and painful business, the first because most do not like to question their acquainted conventions and become a black sheep in the flock, the latter because the light of truth is blinding and confronting. Regarding the inflating cyber-technological dominance, it is not beyond question that the old subsequent idea of "brains in a vat" becomes a matter of fact sooner or later indeed: brains connected to a cyber vat, making the shadows of reality seem real. One might wonder whether this is already the case as we speak - simulating that he went out to buy this book somewhere, the letters of which are just projections of the same letters the author had received from the vat - but then he will end up either as a philosopher, or a village idiot, either a movie maker, or a metal artist.

The latter image of doom is quite unlikely however, not because the vat hypothesis would not be valid, but because plain text is not something future society seems to be willing to promote. Instead of one hundred real - "boring" - pages, being promoted is one digital page small enough to see everything at once on a mini computer, that for the time being is still external to the human body, on which only the shortest sentences with the shortest words underneath the biggest title, together with a prototypical image that pretends to capture "the" meaning, by referring to something everybody already recognizes before he starts "reading". In other words, it is the normalized digital variation for adults of what children from my and previous generations know as "my first book". And one full hour of music of one ensemble without any disruption nor distraction? It does not seem that it will last for another century, knowing that the "development" intends to go faster and faster. Where you could read all artistic and technical information about an album and its use on its sleeves only a few decades ago, you now have to start with hearing or seeing non-related advertisements before a low sound quality file starts to play on a low sound quality device. Who has never heard the real thing, will not notice it is not, so perhaps we are becoming cavemen again after all. Concerned only about shadows and food, to the detriment of soul food, nodding easily yes to a 15 Euro meal produced and consumed within the hour, but no to an album spanning years and never entirely "consumed". The Internet being for music what a gratis bread machine would be for a bakery.

6. Music as media and music as metal

Stereotypically, next to evading musicological and philosophical frames of thinking, an understanding of metal music is seriously being hindered by focusing on only a dozen of bands. The causes can be multiple. Firstly, because the speaker or author has no profound knowledge of other bands. Secondly, because she thinks that understanding the first few bands who got the metal label suffices to understand metal at present. Thirdly, because she thinks that understanding the few bands who are also known by non-metal heads does the trick. Fourthly, because she takes more interest in the bands she likes herself than in (dis)covering the field. Fifthly, because she selects those bands who are to prove a certain point she wishes to make. In each case, metal music is presented with the veil of unity.

These causes are stereotypically part of a bigger vicious circle. Most people only take or seek what can easily be connected to something they already know. Since they never get or ask for an introduction to metal music, they keep on having the wildest ideas about the matter, which prevent them from finding that connection. A typical case of recuperating some sort of connection still, is the metal band that picks up elements that are already claimed by the media establishment and their followers. This can be on the musical level itself, or on levels that do not even have got anything to do with music.

On the first level for instance, by making a cover of a song that fits the criterion, for example "Easy" by (alternative) metal band Faith No More (originally the hit from Lionel Richie with the Commodores). It is highly doubtful that FNM would have had the success they had, if not triggered by this. Even though the song has little to do with their greatest contribution, say the blending of metal, funk and existential elements in thoughtful, dynamic and above all edgy studio and live performances, it brought "the other" FNM under the attention together with a new modest fan base. The strange thing with such a fan base is however that most do not seem to realize that there are much more bands who play (in our case: played) similar music, the main difference just being that they did not hit the charts, and the consecutive means to implement their ideas of course.

On other levels, having a band member already known from TV for instance, is how a metal band is more likely to get appeal from people not declaring themselves as metal heads, more likely than by making groundbreaking music. I happen to have had a customer in my record shop, known from TV as a stand-up comedian, besides being the singer of a metal band. Even though it is clear that the man himself is authentic enough to not want to compromise on the level of his music or music in general, it is clear that his band and metal in general is being noticed by the public more on the grounds of his reputation as a comedian than on any musical grounds. If it would be on musical grounds, there would not be an explanation for the being silent of the common media and takers about legions of other bands who also make very decent music in a similar (Southern/stoner) sub genre. The reception of the metal fans is ambivalent. Some think: "good, finally one of our guys breaking through", while others think: "sad, that there is only attention for metal when it is linked to something other". Indeed, thanks to our customer there was an article about metal in the paper, but it was not part of a broader exploration, neither before, nor after. It is noteworthy that I saw some fresh customers afterwards, yet as soon as they got the album being mentioned in the media - the name or style of which they did not remember - I never saw them back again.

The fact that media do not stand apart from each other, but instead cluster in association with sociological groups, only reinforces the mechanism of subduing musical criteria in favour of sociological ones. In Flanders, a typical cluster of this kind would be Studio Brussel (radio station) - Rock Werchter (music festival) - Humo (magazine) - Woestijnvis (TV company) - De Morgen (newspaper). In between, the spillovers are so ample, that the public is getting an offer that many apparently cannot refuse. Particularly awkward about this cluster is that it pretends to be alternative and even better than the rest, while neither diversity, nonconformity nor thoroughness is obviously on the daily menu. The cluster has quite some success with in the meantime middle aged middle class extroverts who consider themselves progressive. Since mostly the same few people, bands and even jokes are circulating in the cluster, conservative might better cover the picture.

It happens that a band is being hyped and "discovered" by the media cluster and their followers, that fans of metal or musicians-music as such already know for a long time. When it happens, traditionally with a lot of success, one would expect the enthusiasm to spill over to music of the same kind by other names, but no: nothing of the sort. An example in the field of metal could be Mastodon, notwithstanding an honourable band, the products and shows of which all of a sudden being bought by non-metal heads, wishing to remain so out of reasons unknown to us - and perhaps also themselves. Thus, we can only guess a certain conservatism is paying its toll: as metal heads are proud to be fan for life of all of their many favourite bands, media heads are proud to be fan for life of their favourite cluster, accentuated by the many associated gadgets, apps and trends integrated in their life, resulting in being fans of just less bands. One would moreover expect that if Mastodon is not being considered too "hard", which they relatively are within metal, the majority of the other metal bands are also not being considered that way, but no: they are still covered under the dusty label, as if it were some forbidden rotten fruit.

A more local and current example sums up several aspects put above: the band Triggerfinger. They got rather well known here after having covered plain hit parade songs by putting them in a hard rock jacket. In addition, the respectable men have become known from non-specialized magazines, papers, radio and TV programs, where the link with music is not always clear. People seem to accept them, their covers, and their music. At the same time, many programmers, organizers, reporters and new fans do not seem to realize that the music contains a significant portion of early metal, and that it contains in fact less melody, dynamics and clarity than many (other) metal bands. If the people are primarily being concerned with the music, then the big question remains of course: why do many of them not explore other music in the genre, why do they keep on looking at metal heads as alien to them, and why do they keep taking what mainstream media puts on the plate?

The answers are for them to give.

The case gets only more striking with the Belgian band Channel Zero, an exception of a local thrash/groove metal band that received mainstream success here with the teenagers of the nineties, a decade in which metal was relatively more than now present in the common circuit. The band quit in the two thousands and made their come back in the tens. Striking, because it is very straight forward metal actually, and for their come back shows all of a sudden an awful lot of people wanted to be the first ones to get tickets who you do not get to see at any show of any other qualitative thrash band (that is not Metallica). Unlike shows of those other bands, where it seems that you get to see people from the same pool year in year out. People from the Channel Zero come back shows however, were to a significant degree just the ones who happened to be teenagers in the nineties, and perhaps still are, or youngsters fearing to miss out on a possible renaissance of their former popularity, the former in the meantime having become less concerned with music in their daily lives, and primarily taking what is else on the menu of their semi-alternative media. In the shop, they had sooner occasionally come to purchase the following live album containing the songs they already knew, also available in the big chain stores, than noticing the album of an outstanding thrash band that we had playing at the moment, with a discography twice as extensive.

I am sure that much more people would favour this or that metal music, if only they knew about it. But I must immediately add that even knowing something is not doing something. This can be applied to ethics, in the way Aristotle corrected Plato, but also to aesthetics. The music or art may be as beautiful as possible, as long as there is simply no fuss about it, the fuss seldom having anything to do with the art itself, one can only hope for future generations to alter this and take the effort to seek and comprehend the work of art, as if it was your own to create. Next to intrinsically valuable, taking the effort to create it yourself has a useful effect: things that seemed easy become difficult, and things that seemed sensational become dull. As long as the word effort is not generally being associated with culture though - neither from the part of the creator/company, nor from the part of the interpreter/consumer - in favour of mere distraction, entertainment, amusement, "like knows like" and the seemingly harmless illusion of being connected on those grounds, many a piece of music will be in vain.

As we have initiated above, a lot of the few works trying to present metal, stick with bands and styles from "the good old days", like AC/DC, Aerosmith, Black Sabbath, Deep Purple, Iron Maiden, Judas Priest, Kiss, Led Zeppelin, Motörhead, Rush, Scorpions, Van Halen etcetera, and if we are lucky they include some elements from the eighties, like the antagonism "thrashers" (Metallica, Slayer, Megadeth, Anthrax,...) and by the former being called "posers" (Bon Jovi, Mötley Crüe, Poison, Ratt,...). The most obvious problem is that they stop there, while the general styles mentioned only add up for about one twentieth of the current metal landscape, and that the age of few successful bands has made way for the age of many unsuccessful bands.

Also, it needs to be stressed that what are called the first metal bands, did not initially call themselves metal bands. They got the label after the first sides were already composed, and nowadays it seems that some are about to lose it again. The reason for the latter being that what was considered "hard" in 1975, is not that hard in 2015. Pretty much the same with movies: it takes a lot more to display something seen as "sensational" now, than it did 40 years ago. The more people get accustomed to extremes, the more the extreme has to become more extreme in order to have the same effect the next time, when they will be even more accustomed to it, and the spiral continues. Since many assume, for absent reasons, that metal should be as hard as possible, and since the music of old is relatively not as extreme anymore, many of the bands above are considered more rock again than metal.

At the same time, the bands are being re-labeled as rock, because the metal label has become associated with the underground too much and would consequently restrict the market too much. By enclosing the products to the consumers in this way, as if they were not already enclosed, selling rates are enhanced. This is rather ironic, since the most loyal fans of the bands and the genre are metal fans nonetheless. Indeed, metal is mostly in a false way linked to "extremism", while it is not even slightly politically organized, and is more than average particularly sincere about quality music, respect for tradition and authenticity, and would better be linked to "extra-ism". As I am writing, Led Zeppelin's albums are being reissued, and there is an article about it in the lifestyle weekend pages of a newspaper. Yet, who's "expertise" about the music, plainly described as rock, is being asked? That of TV presenters, politicians, common writers, popular musicians,... none of hard rock/metal musicians and connoisseurs.

Another, less obvious, problem is when metal music begins. There seems to be a need among fans and critics alike to put an exact date and location to it, as if before or at the same time on other locations there was no music with metal allures, as if the originators put in their agenda in which week they were to invent metal music, as if any metal music played afterwards was already there more or less, as if this is the only line of the story, and as if metal experts could ever unanimously agree on which moment in the first place. Conferring to some bands named above, there is a tendency to associate "the beginning" with white Englishmen in the seventies, or even eighties when the metal tourist thinks it was too soft back then. I do not see though why there would be less reason to pick a black Afro-American Irish Cherokee in the sixties: Jimi Hendrix. To put it bluntly: guitarists other than hard rock and metal guitarists at present, seem to play like there has never been a Hendrix. Even though this name has by now been encapsulated in mainstream media culture as an icon, the products of which are living a life of there own regardless the original musical and other artistic particularities, the successors of his most important legacy are being bypassed: the virtuosos, the compromise-less, the autodidacts, the value seekers, the gear freaks, the lovers of superlatives, the spectacle makers, the so-called odd ones out, in other words: many a metal maniac. And if Jimi did not have a roadie which he called Lemmy, later front man for Motörhead, things might have turned out rather differently for the genre.

Metal music cannot rightfully be confined though to an appendix of blues music. The instrumentation, as described earlier, the melodic and rhythmical variation, and compositions all out of the blue - only as bonus tracks out of the blues - do not allow for that. In fact, metal music cannot be understood by referring to any single genre. Some metal music can be related to blues, other metal music to another genre. Some metal music can be related to many other genres at the same time, other metal music to its own recent historical development the past half a century or local trademarks. The human brain seems to be fundamentally lazy though: when it sees a relation between things, not only does it want to think it is the only relation, which is wrong in this case, but also does it want to see a cause. When particular (metal) music is being heard, it reminds of something else the brain knows. The less the brain knows, in general or concerning the particular genre, the less it reminds to peer music - in the sub genre(s) of the music, if there is one. Consecutively, the band gets to hear from another one's brain that it is being influenced by a band the former band has never even heard about. This is a classic problem witnessed by musicians vis-à-vis the audience. It is also a classic infringement of the rules of logic: from resemblance, seemingly or not, does not follow that the one should have caused the other.

More generally, music that cannot be at once understood, captured and labeled by one word or sign, is music least probable to get picked up by the multitude. In the mainstream, but in a certain way also within an off-media spectrum that is in itself not simple, like metal. For the best caricatures just seemed to get sold best. This, while it would not be a compliment at all to say to a passionate musician that he is outstanding at being a caricature. While it may serve some social and economic functions, it forgets what is most important: goose bumps, the quite mystical experience of nameless and priceless self-transcendence and self-expression at the very same time.

Another relation, amongst others transgressing the borders of metal as label and the artist's inner world without necessarily being an influence, would be classical music for instance, in general and a Romanticized kind of baroque in particular. The relation is often being silenced, because metal is often being categorized as a form of popular culture, while classical music would not be (lowbrow) popular music but (highbrow) art music. This way of thinking is terribly oversimplifying, and inversely insulting both classical and metal music all at once: uninspired classical music (re)designed for easy consumption by the masses also exists, not as an exception, so it would be an insult for authentic makers of art in the frame of classical music to be placed on the same line; authentic composers-performers of art in the frame of metal music also exist, not as an exception, so it would be an insult for them to be placed on the same line with what we could call pulp metal. Even the latter though is mostly only semi-popular, in the sense that is either popular within the metal community and not outside, or popular outside the metal community and not inside. Generally, even classical music is still much more common to be surrounded by than metal music, and in this sense more popular. In any case, most metal culture does not get the privileges associated with popular culture, nor art culture, in the wide range of publicity. In fact, the word popular alone already bears a negative connotation among metal heads. As we have shown, also metal heads can be prone though to the imperatives of what's hot, trendy and popular at the time in the scene, but if anyone wants to pursue a career in popular music, metal is certainly not the place with the highest chance of success.

Instead of first naming genres, and afterwards putting them as a whole in boxes of popular or not popular music, it would be much more logical, adequate and just to first make the boxes, or rather a gray scale from art (say black) to non-art (white), with popular in the light gray area, and then try to attach separate music - not genres - to the scale. By trying alone, actually pinning is not even necessary, it would become clear that certain classical music and certain metal music are much closer to each other in the dark gray area, than to other classical music and other metal music. I even have the impression that there is an overall negative relation between being a clear example of a genre and obtaining this dark gray position: music that cannot clearly be labeled by or for the public, other than "music", is generally more subtle, demanding and all-influenced, and this just does not seem to sell as good.

Next to resemblances between classical and metal on the level of instrumentation and playing technicality, as we discussed earlier, there are resemblances on the level of writing and styling, and most importantly: the mental world being created by it. Probably the most important things to know about (real) music is, firstly, that it cannot be expressed in any other way, secondly, that it expresses more than what is otherwise being expressed, and thirdly, that what it expresses does not already exist as such before it has been "ex-pressed" as the word would insist. Therefore, talking about the mental content of music, which we could call its essence, is rather absurd. If we were obliged however to put a suggestive word here to describe the main resemblance in this case, it might be: "heaviness". Many talk about heavy metal as if the "heavy" should mean "hard". This is not what "heavy" means though, and "hard" does not represent metal's mental world of music as good as "heavy" in its true sense of "weighing a lot", which is also just a verbal tip of the musical iceberg of course.

In this sense, classical music can also be very, very heavy. At other times it is light decorative background music easily plunging into the daily routine where forced smiles and weather talk avoid any experience of depth challenging the foundations of the bourgeois system. The latter is almost never the aim of metal music though. There are sounds that are on the same continuum as the daily fuss, and there is music. So, when many associate serious music exclusively with (all) classical music and not with metal music, they need to explain us why. On the other hand, music from other genres can be very hard, but this does not mean that it is heavy. Like contemporary dance music. But then it is not so much made to listen to, than to dance to. Rather than heaviness as such or its heavy potential, a musical difference between certain classical and metal would be that the former is more concerned with varying developments of a broad central theme with several endings before the end so it seems, where the latter connects more distinct "finished" themes (riffs) half of which repeated in a hermetic structure.

The supposed distinction between highbrow classical music and lowbrow metal music does not hold either. It is true that less metal fans have a problem with being associated with lowbrow than classical fans would have, but in a subtle way this proves precisely the elitist attitude of the former. When they have no problem with the association, it is not because it is lowbrow, but because it is not-highbrow, in which way they can keep a safe distance from the attributes of status quo authority and chic facades. In fact, many metal heads seem to share an idea of superiority of their own: superior, not based on the traditional standards of highbrow society, but on the belief that "their" music and their (vague) idea of freedom is better. In other words: (self-declared) membership of the metal community is by its members foremost being experienced as membership of the elite, supposedly standing above traditional highbrow. Lowbrow is welcomed, not in the way a union would to overcome the problems raised by the distinction highbrow-lowbrow, but rather to leave the current order behind altogether. In practice, metal musicians and fans come from all layers of society today, and their political views are much more diverse than we and even themselves would think, but most seem to mutually agree on one thing at least: actual politics sounds bad, and a symbolic nay sounds better.

On the level of concerts, two interwoven features makes a standard metal concert quite different from a standard classical concert though. While it seems to be possible to organize a classical concert in a school room for instance without any attention to any decoration, say with one big white TL lamp shining on the performers, audience and furniture alike, this is not something the organizer of a metal show would dare to come out with. Show indeed, because it has this in common with opera also, that theatrical elements are being added to both the set-up and the performance itself. Again, the underlying triangular device seems to be: total controlled expression. The performers thereby having to be able to act to some extent - not as in: to pretend, but as in: to accentuate - contrary to the standard recital, where the person playing barely seems to get involved with the thing being played, giving only attention to the score she hides behind and did not compose herself, preferably being interrupted by a clumsy know-it-all presenter with silly jokes, quite spoiling the musical atmosphere of course.

The second difference then differs also with opera, where the audience - apart from a cough or two, and the undifferentiated applause in the end - tries to be as quiet as possible, and where people remain seated in their reserved chair, worrying about who can claim the arm rests: his neighbour or himself. Less rest and border conflicts at a metal show. The audience is expected to stand up, literally con-centrate and play its part with its neighbours in the big show, not just after, but before, in between and especially in interaction with the playing protagonists. In this sense, it has more in common with African styled high masses. In general, the sociological migration in between all of the three fields (opera fanatics, metal heads and Africans) is as yet surprisingly weak though. Some may fear a metal show for being too expressive physically also. Yes, there might be some boyish "social skirmishing", but this is only part of the game in the front rows, it happens no less at non-seated gigs in other genres, and it is actually not that different from something like rugby without a ball, which seems to be easily tolerated and where injuries are less than with football.

7. Music as metal and the industrial devolution

It is tempting to state that metal originated with workers in industrial cities in England at the dawn of the seventies, and that it is an expression of the metal material associated with the industry, but it would be inaccurate to indulge - like some do, seeking to grant metal mythical powers. For instance, Black Sabbath, Judas Priest and Led Zeppelin happen to be associated with Birmingham, yet not all members came from such a setting inside the city, they never had to work with metal themselves for making a living, and when we compare the sounds metal material makes with the sounds metal music makes there is no significant resemblance. Resemblances do occur within the sub genre industrial metal, but this genre has been developed much later and by other bands. Earlier also, the words "heavy metal" appear in the lyrics of Steppenwolf's hit called Born To Be Wild, the front man for which has German-Canadian roots. In any case, the common utterance of "heavy metal" and "metal" in the musical field did not happen overnight, and the process involved artists, reporters and fans from all sorts of backgrounds. "Heavy metal" had been used outside the musical field of course, for instance in chemistry, military and literature, but there are too few grounds to assume any literal reference. Most plausibly, the figurative associations stimulated by "(heavy) metal" just answered to the growing need for a term to distinguish the music ("metal") and especially the people involved ("metal heads") from the rest, the term itself having become some kind of fetish later on - in sharp contrast with absence of attempt to explore any meaning.

If there is a connection between industrialization and metal culture, it is more likely to have an inverse connection: metal as a medicine to ease the existential pain fed by the increasing demands of machinery, technology, certain economy and mass culture. The industrial revolution, or rather: devolution, reminds of the myth of Pygmalion: man has become dependent on his own inventions, to the point of not being able to live without anymore. Directly or indirectly, the rules are being set either by a demanding machine, an unemployed stockholder or an anonymous multitude. In any case, the time and space left to personalizing humanity/humanizing personality in all its forms (beauty, goodness, truth) is alarmingly minimal, and against any lesson that should have been learned from the ancient Greek intelligentsia. In order to retrieve some sort of human development (arts, philosophy, democracy,...), and at the very same time to denounce the - by now - normal way of life, metal appeals worldwide as an efficient compensation on both accounts.

This is where the 19th century comes in, since when the increase in machines never stopped - be it of decreasing quality (materials, longevity,...) - and since when there have been more world wars, fundamental economic and ecologic crises than anytime before. Some would specify by saying capitalistic crises, in case we may logically wonder though if capitalism ever really existed: capitalism was supposed to mean free markets, and free markets mean - amongst others - many small and independent suppliers with significantly different products and services. Yet, ever since the 19th century, the supposedly free market based system has installed itself in a downward spiral of dependence on few big private suppliers, consequently deciding what is to be bought and at which price (incl. dead weight loss), combined with dependence within the enlarged supply company itself, where the difference between the highest class and the lowest class has widened to the most extreme extents. It is getting no less illogical and cynical to renounce on top of that, that public affairs gets the half of the income, while the highest class gets more than ten times the income distributed to the lowest class, without there being a corresponding total of hours on duty in the week, and with the advantage of holding the power and setting the working conditions - what many would be glad to pay for, if they could, instead of getting paid for. Since I have never heard a capitalist complaining about such (d)evolutions, we may wonder if capitalism is in practice not inherently contradictory indeed.

Now that striving for a monopoly seems to have become the issue then on all accounts, it is furthermore so contradictory to exclude some monopolies, namely states. The capitalist would prefer a private monopoly where he has got nothing to say and where he cannot compete with so it seems, above a public monopoly where he or his ideas could get represented, and without which there would not even be a road leading to any enterprise. The suppliers eventually seek to sell as much as possible at the highest possible price. Yet, they seek to spend as little as possible on the employees or workers and "even" the means, all responsible for the products being products or the services being services. The employees and workers are the biggest part of the demand curve though, so the less they get in return for their sacrificed time, place, independence, critical reflection, higher health risks, important things they could have done otherwise and for their invested efforts to make something out of nothing, by a few means and a lot of procedures set ad hoc mostly by those who never carry out the job themselves, the less demand can be afforded to buy in the first place, or to consume even without buying. As a contradictory consequence, the suppliers seek to have the very same work done by just less direct labour costs, rather than more rationalism, and another downward spiral is in the making.

At the same time we are told that everyone in our capitalistic world is free, as long as he is not in prison. But what is precisely the advantage of being free if you have neither means, power nor climate to do something with it? This is not to say that the happy few who have all are free of course. The Modern dogma seems to be that one is already free when one is free *from* something. But why would one want to be free from something, if it is not to be free *for* something in the end? Perhaps because it is being hoped for that fundamental issues endangering the systemic ideology can be avoided in this way. The question can be avoided why, for instance, people in their "free time" passively watching the same commercial batteries and purchasing accordingly, would be as free as people passionately writing unique metal or other music that will perhaps never be heard, understood nor bought, and yet has an irreplaceable intrinsic value for the one free to do it and perhaps for others as well. The question can be avoided what Modern freedom has got to do with the individual emancipation it initially wanted to be proclaim.

Elaborating all the cultural contradictions involved, would be more than cause enough for another book. You add ecology and Internet, and it would become a voluminous series on recycled paper, that will probably not be read anymore from a till z though. I constrain myself to one more example here, which further - and even literally - inflates the dissonant tone that resonates to the history of ideas and arts. Ever since the 19the century, one has to travel further and further away to not be prone to the denigrating sounds of surrounding machines, electronic devices, commercial radios and so forth. In fact, in so-called normal Western way of life it is not possible anymore to function without having to hear ample ugly noises. However, this is contradictory to the core idea of the original liberals, agreeing with the saying that the right to swing your fist ends where my nose begins. In other words: the right to wave your noise ends where my ear begins. However, this right is being infringed pretty constantly, primarily even by those who dare to call themselves liberal. The inconsistency does not stop here. Radios in public and even strictly professional areas, and in private areas sounding through other private or public areas: who complains about the infringement is being looked at as if she came from Mars, even though man on Earth has spent 99,99% of all time without it, and if she proposes classical or "even worse" metal music instead - provided that the radio "has to" remain - she becomes public enemy number one. Advertisements, commercial music, electronic tunes, motorized tools,... nobody is supposed to complain about it, but metal music played at a lower decibel level even, and the police will not be far away. Mobile ringing being often the only way in which people get in contact with what once was classical music.

The consequences for the welfare, well-being and self-control of humanity based on such a system are severe and quite silently taken for granted. On the cultural level, it has one paradoxical advantage though: the inflammation of a Romantic reaction, not only in the 18-19th century but also as we speak. It seems that the tensions that cannot be expressed and synthesized through the system, seek compensation through art. The word romantic bears a lot of connotations, yet few are faithful to romantic with a capital R as occurred and occurring in the arts and music in particular.

A first misinterpretation can as best be called the Valentine's Day interpretation. Romantic music has got less to do with the latter though than a plain urban pop song has. The "I luv u babe" again and the importunate marketing on all levels at the time, make it precisely more a token of systemic immanence than transcendence. Of course, love plays an important part in Romantic music, as hate does by the way, but in the narrow way of avoiding superficiality and economy and letting in both the extreme and the ambivalent.

A second misinterpretation is to connect it with Rome or the Roman languages and cultures. While it is true that ancient Rome can be a great source of inspiration for the Romantic artist, greater than for other artists, the same counts for ancient Greece, Egypt or Scandinavia for instance. At the same time, speaking or being Germanic - not necessarily German - is no impediment to be Romantic. I would even say that Germanic Romantics are relatively the most numerous on the level of music, both classical and metal. Perchance because the industrialization took off in their backyard. On top of that, Romanticism has much more to do with the medieval romance, say the post-Roman era. While some trace back King Arthur for instance to ancient Rome, it is primarily in its medieval or neo-medieval interpretation that many a Romantic has found both means and end to his artistic and existential quest.

A third misinterpretation is to connect Romanticism with anti-rationalism. This is of course the easy way out for those not willing or capable to explain why non-Romanticism would be rational. Indeed, the deeper problem is not that Romanticism would not be rational, but that it gives reasons to criticize the dominant yet implicit Modern ideas or rather illusions of rationality. To discuss Modernity as such, takes a whole library. In brief, I mean the era here that willingly neglects insights from classical antiquity, the Middle Ages and the Renaissance, and finds its culmination in the industrial, technocratic, mechanized, quantified and dual society of few wolves and many sheep of the past few centuries. While most metal heads are actually sheep in wolf's clothing, today's biggest wolves wear white-collar sheep's clothes. As we have already indicated, the imposed way of life - dictated by demagogic mass mechanisms of pointless inventions and backstage investors - produces many contradictions, making us wonder whether it is as rational as it pretends to be, and whether it should be considered the only or at all reasonable way. And it is precisely the opposite: because there are so many contradictions, tensions and disappointments, instead of reasons, that the Romantic seeks to compensate for his loss of humanity, and its most distinctive feature: reason, on other accounts. The anti-Romantic values of mass production, disposable materialism, short-term egotism, hollow hedonism and utilitarianism for the happy few, have much more to do with impulses and instincts in fact, than with anything reasonable, qualitative and ...knightly. Being critical and creative are reasonable features par excellence. Computers lack them, so the late industrial obsession to computerize everything and everyone does far from prepare an evolution still.

The virtuosity, heaviness, scope and depth present in Romantic music, classical and metal alike, is in challenging contrast of course to the superficial homogeneity of often superfluous artificiality and to the worrying casualness currently promoted in industrial, professional and even artistic products, styling and language. One might as well say: while the arts have been contaminated with Modern industry, the products of non-industrial craftsmen alone were already more worthy of the name art. While keeping up the "standard" could refer to a qualitative discourse, Modern man implicitly chooses every day to restrict himself to quantitative aspects - say standardization - in keeping up what is supposed to be "norm-al". Keeping up what does not add any value, is equal to keeping up nothing however. Again, the contradiction could not have been bigger: the first minute Modern man promotes his personal individuality, particularity and liberty, the next minute he just takes whatever the standardization process has put on the plate.

On top of the standardization, comes specialization. Not in the sense for instance that a dress in an H&M store in country X would be different from a dress in an H&M store in country Y, but in the sense that almost no one can say anymore: today I sold the dress that I made last week. Instead, dozens of people have to get involved from all corners of the world to just make one single dress and sell it. Instead of being the master of the process from alpha to omega, one has to find satisfaction as a human being with only attaching buttons for instance, day in day out, or with driving thousands of kilometres, night in night out, because both wages together can still be kept lower than the minimum wage, and health and safety conditions not met. Also, other than with the (gone) dressmaker in the nearest village, durable quality and personal style is seldom the result, but why does this matter if the buyers only plan on wearing something for the season in which it is considered hot and trendy? If that is what they need at all, when they go shopping just for the fun they think they are going to have with it. Consumers, producers, non-producing managers and so-called shareholders alike are getting involved in a process where no one knows anymore who precisely does what precisely, and more and more energy is being wasted as a consequence of the vacuum created where no one knows anymore how precisely to change anything. In the face of history, it is quite recent actually that people are expected to have only one narrow occupation in their short lives. Only over a century ago, a musician could as well be a priest, a general teacher or whatever, and within the music, a performer as well as a composer, a pianist as well as an organist, etcetera. Once you realize that life is short enough indeed, then music has also a better chance of becoming music again.

As if it is life, to be split into a mind-numbing job to survive at the one hand, and so-called free time or relaxation on the other hand. Music and culture in general has got nothing to do with both. Animals, and perhaps humans sooner or later, do not do metal because they are only busy surviving, and metal is not just some means to relax as good as any other, say a massage machine, but an effort towards a meaningful cultural space. Where the daily device seems to be to multi task as much as possible and as fast as possible, and to stay within the space of what is concretely given, artistic evolution is best helped with taking as much time as possible for forgetting about means and concentrating on meanings, in a space that is thereby created.

One might find some resemblances of these writings to the writings of Theodor Adorno and Walter Benjamin, associated with the Frankfurter Schule/Critical Theory around the interbellum. As far as I know their works, there seems to be only one resemblance though: deeply worrying about the commodification and banalization of art. Neither of them was concerned with metal music of course, nor as such with where we might find metal "avant la lettre": heavy classical, technical blues, amplified folk,... Jazz however, the current nonconformity and musicianship of which is getting respected by quite a few metal musicians, received a great deal of Frankfurter critique - witnessing its highest popularity. While my principle is to make the arts in general and music in particular as autonomous as possible, Adorno in particular tends to refrain from capitalistic spillovers indeed, in favour of yet another set of rules though, like the twelve-tone system, atonality and randomness, not really caring about how the music sounds in the end, by focusing on the novelty of the underlying pattern as such. In the eyes of music alone though, it does not matter how new something is, how awkward, how intellectual, how spontaneous or how... As pointed out earlier, music does not have anything to do with any dictionary word actually, but with music's own language, that we could at the most report as being more or less "sublime". Since atonality for instance is seldom being sought nor found in metal music, and since the Apollonian aspects of the latter make it often bend towards overwhelming tonality even, it is quite unlikely that Adorno would have favoured the genre, even though the critical potential of metal is much bigger than that of jazz at the time. Paradoxically, it is to be remarked that whoever does not try to be original or to be anything, the abundant inward musical inspiration being her sole guide, has precisely a bigger chance of ending up as someone bringing not only original music, but also sublime.

To not let music be dictated by anything other than music, allows for plural forms of pluralism: not only will there be more room for inner diversity within the music itself, and the recognition thereof, there will also be more room for diversity in between the different spheres of human life, of which music is one. With "spheres" there is a wink to Michael Walzer's book "Spheres of Justice, A Defense of Pluralism and Equality" (1983). Although he wrote about almost all spheres but art and music, it would not be too far-fetched to extrapolate the basic intuition. Pluralism, not so much as an aim in itself than as a consequence of giving every sphere its due, by watching that the proper economic, religious, political, familial,... or artistic workings do not colonize the other - thereby articulating systemic inequality and injustice. I would also add that this theoretical framework is more complex and adequate than the neo-Marxist bifurcation of the economic sphere and the cultural sphere, even though it is obvious that in practice the economic sphere - in itself the outcome of an implicit ideology I would say - is colonizing the other spheres to the largest extent nowadays, and has in silence even internally abandoned the "liberal" ideology of free markets with the most plural supply and demand as discussed.

Karl Marx and Richard Wagner passed away in the very same winter of the year 1883. We may symbolically regard upon this date, certainly not as the defeat, but instead as the getting underground of the most substantial (Western) critiques of the dominant liberal conception of the discredited humanities, where less politics is regarded as better politics, where the production and consumption of art is regarded as not any different from factory biscuits say, where philosophy is regarded as either harmful, or waste of time and money, and where history does not have its place, and future neither so it seems. No surprise then, that it has steadily become a commonplace for metal fanatics to guess that if Wagner lived today, metal would be quite his cup of tea. The Romantics, the heaviness, the bombast, the complexity, the eccentricity, the drama, the poetry, the visuals, the edge, the cinematic "avant la lettre",... it is all there. Strange though that metal fans seem to realize this better than classical fans do as yet.

There is a simple trick to find out what many still believe to be difficult: the overlap of metal and classical music, far from limited to Wagner and the Romantics. Take a piece of classical music, let it be played with the instrumentation as described earlier, and it will be considered metal-among-other-metal in quite some cases, by an audience of course that does not know it was classical. Vocals, bass and percussion for their respective parts, distorted guitar in particular suit to play the leading themes, in practice much more suit than acoustic guitar actually - that has a much more resembling approach in flamenco for instance than in its rather poor classical presence - and keyboard for remaining orchestration.

Or, in reverse, take a piece of metal music, let it be played by classical instruments, and it will be considered classical-among-other-classical in quite some cases, by an audience unbiased. The latter formula has already been used by the band Apocalyptica for instance. Cellos instead of metal guitars say, and if you would not know that an original metal composition is being covered, you would probably think of it as decent classical music.

Literal examples of the first formula are rather fragmentary. While there is no band that I know of yet that puts the oeuvre as such of Antonin Dvořàk for instance in a metal jacket, there is the band Rhapsody (of Fire) for instance, that has integrated themes from Dvořàk, and a lot of other classical composers, in its metal songs. In general, the works of Antonio Vivaldi, Johann Sebastian Bach (not the painter), Ludwig van Beethoven, Niccolò Paganini, Franz Liszt, Edvard Grieg, Richard Strauss, Sergei Prokofiev and other composers with a hint of me(ga)lomania, willing to go over the top in terms of what is being called shred (virtuosity), bombast or stubbornness, are also relatively popular to wink to in metal compositions, appearing in the thanks to section of the album booklet, being discussed as "which one is the most metal?" in various metal web fora, etcetera. But also when no reference to anything already existing is there, some music might as well be described as the spirit of symphonic, Romantic, barok, old,... music with other means, instead of metal music. And this is no exception: the tags symphonic, orchestral, operatic, neoclassical, neomedieval, "gothic"... flavoured metal form a well-established family within the metal community.

Again, a sticker on the CD displaying "Symphonic Melodic Metal" helps to sell to the metal fans, whereas a sticker on a classical CD displaying "Metallic Heavy Classical" is neither ordinary, nor recommended marketing wise probably vis-à-vis the classical fans, who mostly seem to choose to be blind for any resembling inspiration. Moreover, when we say melodic metal, we actually say a pleonasm, because the majority of metal music is indeed highly melodic compared to most other genres. Personally, I admit, this was the main reason for me in the first place to start digging into metal music as a teenager, at the time listening to Megadeth and the Beach Boys on the same evening, for quite the same appetite. A decade later, Dave Mustaine (the front man and founder of Megadeth, after he was put out of Metallica) declared in an interview that he was a fan of the Beach Boys, so the parallel is not as crazy as most did assume back then. This is also where the marketing and mediatization comes in again: bands get a steady profile, in metal traditionally a hard profile, in the end often not having to do too much with the music itself anymore. Especially non-metal fans usually overestimate the hardness and sameness of metal bands, and underestimate the hardness and sameness of their own favourite bands, DJ's or streaming app. And where can we find the best power ballads after all?

8. Maps and traps

Different metal bands play different metal music, and it would take a full-time job to just count the metal bands worldwide. Also, within one metal band severe differences can occur between their albums, between their songs and even within one song. To the point that to define a song as a metal song, is neither as simple as it might seem, nor as adequate. The assumption that there exists some sort of an approved criterion today to decide what is metal music and what is not, is simply false. The many who assume such, do not seem able to explain "the criterion". A suggestive criterion is theoretically possible though, but either it would be so abstract that it is hollow, or it would be made concrete but constantly prone to critique, or the detailed content (for example relatively a lot of distortion, double bass,...) would be contrasting with the undetailed image of metal, the music of which is not even made distinct and general analysis absent or unconscious. From the most important point of view: artistic liberty, it would also be counter-productive.

Endorsed with the instrumental and vocal peculiarities as described earlier, there are many different ways to make metal music: the composing, songwriting, performing and overall styling can take many forms, both consecutively and simultaneously. We could call these forms sub genres. The notion of sub genre is not unproblematic when applied to metal music though. A sub genre usually hints that, firstly, a/one genre exists encompassing all the sub genres, secondly, that the "sub-genre" is subordinate to the genre, thirdly, that the sub genres are clearly distinct, fourthly, that a band belongs to a/one (sub) genre. However, it is the genre that belongs to the band, not otherwise. Even bands themselves sometimes forget this. Judas Priest initially never intended to play heavy metal and become the metal gods they have become. Their first album Rocka Rolla back in the seventies, has got more to do with what the title suggests indeed than with metal music or heavy metal music, even though the metal community later on claimed it as "theirs" (and theirs alone). The band does not belong exclusively to Rock 'n Roll either, noting how their edgy sound has grown every decade more so.

Of course, it is against popular marketing to not present a band as a/the representation of a certain (sub) genre, and of course there is more sociological magic to identify with a certain label (I do not mean record label), but the musicological and artistic truth is very different. The music that bands make is mostly a combination of all sorts of genres, and examining which precisely is more likely to lead to discussions than to beautiful harmony - both outside and inside the band. Also, the contradiction is to be noted when bands intend to imitate a certain band, Judas Priest for instance, and then try to copy their sound whilst playing somewhat different compositions. If they wanted to imitate properly, they would have to think: we are not going to confine ourselves to this or that genre, and make whatever music we find ourselves inspired to. This is how Priest became artistically, sooner than economically, big in the first place. Or, if The Beatles had decided to form an a capella band just like the Beach Boys, they would never have become pioneers themselves. Still, it is clear that The Beatles would not be The Beatles without the Beach Boys, but their freedom of mind paved the way for a song like Revolution, which has quite some metal "influences" actually, apart from the long hair.

I know it would be easier to just draw a pyramid with metal on top, the sub genres in the middle, under which the respective bands. The pyramid would have a holy allure, and animated posters of it would make a good selling. The problem however is that it would not correspond to reality. It would paradoxically also have destructive effect, since it would only encourage the caricature that is being made of metal music, preventing the music to be taken seriously, recognized and fully developed. The pyramid encloses itself, thereby forgetting that without spillovers from what is called classical music, rock, punk, gothic, folk, blues, psychedelia, jazz, country and - yes - pop, funk, rap and even techno, there would not be much left actually of the things that are called metal music, and vice versa. The more you try to trace back the music of a certain metal band, the more you wonder in the end whether you could call it just a metal band indeed. More rule than exception, the music can be interpreted as a combination of sub genres, that are being redefined as they are being played, not residing under metal alone, and dynamically reintegrating musical flavours, some of which have become a genre and others who have not or not yet. As metal music had been invented before there was "metal music", it is being invented ever after.

Oversimplifying then, to give newcomers an idea, we might tell that metal went through the gradual process of discovering itself (sixties-seventies), consolidation and golden age (eighties), fragmentation and mainstream issues (nineties), regrouping and deepening (two thousands), music industry crisis and widening (tens). The year 1991 is broadly associated indeed with the fact that until then things went better and better in metal, both with regard to the total amount of sales in general and the satisfaction of the metal community in particular, never retrieved afterwards as we speak. Around that time, many experienced bands saw revenues declining while very few went in the opposite direction of Hollywood status, probably due to the getting more popular of other (sub) genres like grunge and alternative rock/metal. Quite many bands tried to change their style into a more promising direction, but the result was mostly the opposite: while the fans of the first hour felt deceived by what they interpreted as "gone mainstream", an equally valid fan base was not gained in return. While I think that, from a musicological and aesthetic point of view, a lot of interesting paths were taken though, it only seemed to work for the happy few. Other bands did their best to the contrary to sound as inaccessible as possible, thereby entering the underground from which only a dozen were ever able to rise again in full daylight.

There never was much unity in metal though other than in people's heads, but around the nineties quite separate families within the metal community were more inclined to live a life of their own. The biggest ones were, and still are to a large extent, in no particular order: (a) traditional heavy metal, hard rock; (b) thrash metal, speed metal; (c) Album/Adult Oriented Rock, glam metal; (d) power metal, progressive metal; (e) death metal, grindcore; (f) black metal, pagan metal; (g) doom metal, dark metal; (h) alternative metal, metalcore. A handful of - random - examples might be, respectively: (a) Accept, Iron Maiden, Judas Priest, Thin Lizzy, UFO; (b) Anthrax, Flotsam And Jetsam, Megadeth, Metallica,

Slayer; (c) Europe, Fate, Poison, Ratt, Survivor; (d) Dream Theater, Helloween, Rhapsody (of Fire), Stratovarius, Yngwie J. Malmsteen imitators; (e) At The Gates, Cannibal Corpse, Death, Morbid Angel, Napalm Death; (f) Bathory, Cradle Of Filth, Falkenbach, Dimmu Borgir, Immortal; (g) Candlemass, Cathedral, Funeral, My Dying Bride, Pentagram (h) Biohazard, Faith No More, Heaven Shall Burn, Killswitch Engage, System Of A Down. Any sub genre could again be more or less artificially be divided into several sub genres, thereby also crossing the sub genre, and the possible examples - only together covering the load - are so ample and each associated with a whole atmosphere, that it is just impossible to give away a few without hurting someone's feelings actually.

Stylistically then, there is this paradox: how "normal" it becomes in the end to recognize a piece of metal music as this and/or that sub genre, so difficult it is to explain in words to the untrained ear. While (b) is explicitly influenced by aforementioned (a) in general, and the so-called New Wave Of British Heavy Metal in particular, it definitely differs in the rhythm and guitars having much more speed, punch and hooks, the vocals having become most exclaiming and the lyrics most ominous. Notable differences occur between so-called new school and old school thrash - often wrongly spelled as trash - and within the old styled between US and EU, and between West Coast and East Coast US. Visually, short pants and high-top sneakers have nowhere else been as stylish. Actually, (b) is heavier than what goes by the name of heavy metal as a sub genre. Relatively the most light of all is (c), where the main focus is to produce, according to some "overproduce", the catchiest songs, without giving in on excellent musicianship and rough edges though. Even when the bands do not come from the eighties or the US, they often elaborate an eighties-US-like filmic atmosphere, therapeutic and spirits up. Nowhere else look the men so much like women, instead of the other way around. It has in common with (d) that melody is a top priority, but while for (c) more is less, for (d) more is ...more. A certain *horror vacuity* paves the way here for remarkably technical, wide-ranging, accelerating and powerful epics indeed, especially in the German, Northern European and more and more Mediterranean variants. The themes, lyrical and visual alike, make an almost aristocratic blend of the heroic, the historic and the cosmic.

Notwithstanding that melodic and/or technical death metal also proudly falls under the umbrella of (e), (e) is overall particularly rough: blastbeats, down-tuned guitars, grunting vocals, primordial extravaganza,... If we are to use the word aggressive, now would be the least inconvenient time. Straightforward as these men usually are, they are probably the ones who spend the least time in front of the mirror of all. Together with (f), it is the most extreme sub genre. Black 'n death would probably be in the top three of Scandinavia's biggest export products overall. However, (f) is far less concerned with technical differentiation and innovation than (e), often sticking to a combination of drums barely catching up with the fast unmuted string pulling and shrieking vocals, altered with spherical passages, in favour of representing the feeling of blackness and cultivating the imagination of heathenism in all its possible aspects. While (g) is also more about feeling, it is particularly slow and low, and - apart from some Black Sabbath imitators - least attached to calculated musical patterns and ditto showing off, to the benefit of varying walls of sounds revoking holy or unholy serenity, existential depression and ritualistic mysticism.

Perhaps because of the same reason, namely feeling, women seem to be relatively quite attracted to (f) and (g). Quite contrary to (h), which is most down to earth of all, and where consequently more urban elements find there place, along with people more young and ...black. Different styles, regardless of how metal they are supposed to be, are explicitly incorporated to bring to life surprising grooves of the revolutionary sort. A few derivative bands have been deprecatingly called nu-metal by fans of other metal. When I was closing down the shop, deathcore sold relatively the most within "the" metal map, which is theoretically the result of a certain combination of (e) with (h) though.

The different flavours are not restricted to the music itself: when I only saw a metal head entering the shop, I could already correctly deduct in most occasions which musical style or styles were his cup of tea. This has got less to do with me, than with many metal heads working hard at giving a right first impression, rather than a good or a bad one. It is only a minority, including myself, who does in his spare time not actively seek to be an expert at giving this or that metal appearance, or a metal appearance tout court. The reasons for this can differ though. Some just do not like to go through the fuss again they are getting into by being seen as a metal head by non-metal heads, others like too many different styles to specialize in a certain look, some do not find the metal clothes and accessories very functional and comfortable, still others are less concerned with material things like clothes altogether than with spiritual things like music. Nonetheless, the metal merchandise market is quite a big one, both in supply and in demand, and as I am writing, more and more bands are saying that they get more income from their merchandise than from their music. As a rather alienating twist, it happened indeed that a client of mine was asking for an introduction into the music of the band she was already proudly wearing a shirt of.

Of course, it seems to be a good way for promotion and recognition to wear a band shirt at first sight. However, if a common man sees someone passing with the metal shirt, he is not acquainted with the band's oeuvre, nor does it make him do research on it, so he keeps on having false associations, which does not help the band nor metal in general any further, nor does it help to understand the one who is wearing it at all. If the spectator is a fellow metal head, he decides for himself which bands he privileges as well, so the status quo remains also here. It is not as easy as with football shirts for instance, from which you can deduct the football team of which region is being stated, accentuating the opposition of the supporters of the one team against the other. Regional machismo and opposition between metal bands is not the issue though. If there can be talk of opposition, it would rather be between metal as such and the popular rest. But no matter how much shirts are being worn and seen, it will not make the spirit itself that it refers to any more public, so every social group stays within his cocoon. When the mirror image of metal as direct visual identification, materialism and economic behaviour lives a life of its own, the connection is blurred with both the inner meanings and the contribution to an integral symbolic order communicated in musical, reflective or other cultural ways. The books of Jacques Lacan and Jürgen Habermas can shed more light upon these mechanisms.

Merchandise, band shirts, long sleeves, cut-off sleeves, girlies, tank tops, hoodies, worker shirts, baggy pants, jackets, vests, capes, black colours, pale skins, leopard themes, leather, denim, stretch, spandex, corsets, shorts, belts, horns, boots, hi-top sneakers, stilettos, caps, hats, scarves, bandanas, patches, buttons, spikes, pins, rivets, studs, rounds, chains, necklaces, armbands, bracelets, ruffed cuffs, gauntlets, rings, piercings, make up, tattoos, hair(un)dressing, föhn, beard experimentation, bodybuilding, posters, flags, bags, purses, mugs, glasses, calenders, accessories, decorations, housewares, bed linen, logos, gadgets, stickers, banners, pagan symbols, religious, chivalric signs, Celtic, Saxon, Viking, Nordic mythology, Western, glitter, pink, red, purple, burlesque, horror, bullets, battle gear, military wear, biker, gothic, punk, aristocratic, lolita, Elisabethian, Victorian, mourning, emo, retro, neglectful in a studied way, the (static) posture, the metal greeting (shaking the thumb instead of all the other fingers), the way of walking even (legs wide and shoulder down when foot placed)... the list of the visual metal (re)styled landscape is almost infinite, both concerning the levels of appearance and the ways of appearance. Almost, because the metal image building seems to encompass about everything but what is fashionable at the time with the local urban franchisee of the biggest chain store. Although, as I am speaking, this is no longer true in a certain way. For instance, it has become generally fashionable right now to wear all sorts of clothing with studs. This results in self-declared metal heads, literally, blaming supposedly fake-metal heads for wearing their tokens. Of course, this poses an as yet unanswered question: if the difference made between fake and true metal heads does not depend on the outer tokens, then why does a metal head take so much time, and money, to dress up in the first place? And, to the metal outsiders: when a classical performer for instance dresses as black as a metal head, which he almost always seems to do nowadays, then why does he "get away with it" while the metal head is being stigmatized because of it?

The different stylings, different both in the way of mutually different and together different from mainstream expectations at the time and place, are prone to changes of course during time, but compared to other fashions quite traditional. Many metal heads still want to look precisely like their gods who flourished in the eighties. The most obvious changes however are that black ware has become more dominating indeed, that short haircuts have become more acceptable and that the remnants of hippie patterns have severely diminished altogether. Analogue to the music, stylings can be grouped to a certain extent. Insiders have a frame of categories in their brain so to speak, with which they perceive and construct the metal appearances automatically. In order to make it clear to outsiders, let us use an example that most people (in the Western world) know about: the Lord of the Rings, both the original books by J.R.R. Tolkien and the films by Peter Jackson. The trilogy has become widely popular, and even more so in the metal community. It is clear that the (heavy) themes themselves, the (Romantic) ways of presenting them and the (demanding) elaboration of the whole, form the perfect inspiration for metal fans and artists worldwide, even though the overall non-related commodification later on did not suit its original authenticity. Paradoxically, while the work is said to be neomedieval, I doubt whether the books could ever have been written the way they have only a century earlier: before the expats on all fronts of the Industrial Revolution, the first Great Depression and the first two World Wars, which it subtly articulates and criticizes at the same time.

A lot of references have always been made from the metal band names, the lyrics and the visions, to the books of Tolkien. Nobody seems to know who started it, but the different characters in the movie trilogy are even being compared to the different characters in metal. Of course, this is no exact science, but conferring to a few pages back, we could come up with something this: (a) Théoden, (b) Orcs, (c) Legolas, (d) Aragorn, (e) Uruk-hai, (f) Nazgûl, (g) Dead Men of Dunharrow, (h) Gollum. Concerning the sub-sub genres, we could further associate the Hobbits with folk metal, Gimli with viking metal, Arwen with female fronted gothic metal, Gandalf the White with white/Christian metal, Saruman with symphonic metal and so forth. Interestingly enough, the actor Christopher Lee (°1922) who played the role of Saruman, has actually made a symphonic metal album (Charlemagne) a decade after the movies, besides being invited as a guest singer for other projects in the scene. His strong reputation for bringing to life the darkest parts, together with his imposing voice and efforts to play from the cradle till the grave, all makes this old maverick highly respected in the metal community. The most bridging character in general seems to be Boromir, as played by Sean Dean at the pictures. The fact that his (evenly tragic) role later on as Eddard Stark in the successful TV series Game of Thrones, based on the books "A Song of Ice and Fire" by George R.R. Martin, received wide acclaim and sympathy from metal fans, only adds to this.

In global, there has been some sort of a revival of the fantasy genre and historical or theatrical epos since the two thousands indeed, encompassing different cultural products like pictures, (comic) books, board games, computer games, role playing, re-enactment even,... but in metal there has always been such a revival actually. Importantly, while fans of metal music are often also fans of these other cultural domains, the almost mainstream revival does not seem to work "in reverse" though: even though others now like to identify with characters like the above and overall styling, metal music itself remains undercover, and awareness of (significant) commonplaces with the extended metal field unexpressed. Likewise, when there was a tendency with metal artists around the beginning of the new millennium to focus on their core business and often literally regroup, after a decade of more experimentation and consequently fragmentation, this did not really have anything to do with forces coming from outside the metal community.

Now, in the two thousand and tens, it seems that the pouring out of the most common sub genres in numerous variations has made more way, not so much for experimentation, than for combining elements from several sub genres within metal music. The squaring of sub genres will of course result into an even more complex landscape. The fans of the niche find yet another name for it, and already at this point, the one listening to one kind of metal has no idea anymore what the other is listening to. Contrary to popular belief, the one extreme has indeed nothing to do anymore with the other. This is furthermore enhanced by the fact that quite everything has become more optional, individual and anonymous at the same time: instead of getting acquainted with all sorts of metal (fans) or other music (fans), in public places like record shops or pubs, one can as well shut herself off with headphones through which only the tracks or even seconds chosen on her computer, or more and more by her computer.

While it might have been true that metal was a youth culture until the eighties, it would be wrong to still associate metal with youth as many outsiders do. The fans and artists from the eighties have become thirty years older now, and the vast majority has not abandoned metal for good. Indeed, more than other cultural spheres, metal does not seem to be something you feel like doing just for the summer, but something that becomes part of your life from discovery to the grave, or does not become a part at all. The longer the person has been involved in metal, the more he is respected as "true" both by his peers and himself, on the basis of commitment as well as knowledge. This in contrast to the current tendency in our society to treat someone like a little child the older he gets. Also, the newest fans of the genre are not always the youngest fans. It takes time, money and independence to do research on metal, and young students do seldom enough have this. When youth is getting into metal, the visual aspects seem to prevail at first nowadays - above the auditive aspects. I have known many youngsters collecting a full metal outfit, the auditive references from which not (yet) occurring in their memory. This has less to do with metal youth however, than with a society in which visuals and the recognition based thereon, claim far more attention than any sound wave. That I witnessed that, in my shop, the older were mostly more interested, that fathers and sons often came for the music together, and that metal concerts have become more of a family event, only affirms my understating that metal is a youth culture.

Metal is also often named a subculture. This can be interpreted in contradicting ways though. "Sub" could mean, firstly, below something (culture) without being a branch of it, or, secondly, a branch of something (cultural). "Culture" could mean here, firstly, not a culture in itself because it is below, or, secondly, a cultural branch. Many possibilities thus, but none is able to cover the load of metal without misunderstandings. Metal is a culture, and even form of art, not as a substance but as a verb, that has connections with a variety of other cultures through time and space, without being a mere branch of something - what would this particular thing be? - willingly or not at odds with current mainstream culture, if we may call the latter culture in the way in which we call art culture. For this, and reasons that we explicitly discussed earlier, we also cannot just call it pop(ular) culture.

Still others call metal a counter culture, also without explaining themselves. Who says "counter", has to say counter "X" though. If X is "culture", then metal would not be culture. What would it be then instead? Nature? I do not think so. If X is something else, then something else needs to be explained. If it is not being explained, the illusion is kept alive that metal is against everything. If metal would be against everything, then it would also be against itself, which it is not, it would be against all the other cultures that are against something, which it is not, and foremost it would be against all the other forms of art that are actively sought to incorporate in the metal world, which it is not. If something has to be called a counter culture, it should be the established culture, generally cultivating a bias counter metal, but also counter traditional folk, non-classical classical music, jazz,... and counter philosophy, history, qualitative sociology, rational criticism, (display of) material poverty and much more.

Whereas the few who discuss metal first start with posing which culture it is or not, I propose to do the opposite: to first start discussing metal, and only then to consider associative nouns. Our analysis has shown that metal is not as simple as sorting litter, even though the latter has become not always very clear also. While it is possible to determine whether a material is wholly or partly metal though, and dispose of it accordingly, it is neither possible nor meaningful to do this with metal culture. To make culture a basket is in itself an attack on culture. A culture that is not intrinsically arguable and has no differentiation in time and place, in other words: that is not continuously being reinvented by people of flesh and blood, is a culture that does not exist. Consequently, the exclusiveness of cultures is more about window dressing than reality. Metal, both its music and its imagery, is a multitude of ways of expressing and generating human thoughts and feelings, and in this way never straight from a beginning till an end, but always combinations of widening, deepening, narrowing, paving, repairing, neglecting, descending, rising, turning, bridging, crossing, merging with other ways, parting from,...

That metal is above all an international affair, more than any other genre perhaps, spanning the globe from Finland over Japan to Brazil, constructing quite the same spectrum of demand and supply, accentuates that it is primarily about universal human perspectives on standing-in-the-world, not from this or that particular group. While football is also an international affair, it is actually just about the winning or not of this or that particular region or nation, not about the kind of brotherhood shared by all metal heads. The football fan may look more sympathetic and conformist, but on the level of aggression, the biggest metal festival cannot compete with the smallest football match. Also, the biggest metal festival gets less attention by the conventional media than the smallest football match. And everybody is delighted when people wear during their job two red horns on the top of their head when the Belgian football club, the Red Devils, are in playing season, but if someone wears a metal T-shirt with devil artwork at work, bad remarks are the response. Who is then exclusive after all?

While metal is mostly an underground phenomenon, meaning that the conventional channels are not open for it, some interesting regional differences occur. Scandinavia and especially next to it: Finland, is the region with relatively (to population) the most metal artists and fans. Even though the metal music from there is not particularly more accessible or easy than in other parts of the world, and often even extreme as black or death metal, it is less underground. Metal songs do have a chance to be included in the overall Hit Parade, or even the Eurovision Song Contest, and if not audible, metal is visible in almost every street in town. A portrait of the special case of Finland has been extensively documented on the DVD "Promised Land of Heavy Metal", directed by Kimmo Kuusnimi, 2008.

Also in other countries, for example Germany, Japan, Chile, metal is more prominent than in others, for example Mauritania, Afghanistan, Cambodja. What interests us most here is the reason why. Many metal heads enjoy to come up with the wildest Viking-like ideas, but as far as I know Vikings never played metal music. Alcohol consumption is another parameter easily used, but why then not just stick to Russian folk? And why then were common people more interested in the mead that I made than in the metal music that I made? The climate, and long nights in particular, might be more relevant than it appears at first: not so much because the darkness is reflected by the music - it would be more plausible to compensate by making the lightest music - but because there are just less other things to do on a long and cold night at home, than to concentrate on a complicated piece of music, instead of another game of football with the gang on the street for instance.

Richard Florida, an American urban studies theorist, recently claims to have gathered empirical evidence for three common hypotheses online: the more metal in a country, firstly, the more welfare in the country, secondly, the more musical education by the state, thirdly, the more tolerance by the people. This might indeed explain why metal seems to occur least around the equator, where welfare is probably the most hard to find now, and why it not only occurs more in the wealthy north, but also in the far south of all continents. Of course, the less you have to be concerned about getting your daily bread, water and shelter, the more you can afford art. Musical education is in northern Europe indeed the most subsidized and promoted by the state, and quite likely also the most enhanced, and about one third of the children there are having such an education. Since most metal music demands an above average insight in music, this reason is also not too far-fetched. To be a metal head is the most difficult and even dangerous in Islamic countries. The interest in metal grows there every day though, and most of the few academic writing is about the relation of metal with Islam even, but general lack of tolerance makes it as underground as possible, so this too has an explanatory advantage.

Nonetheless, toleration, self-criticism and rationalism is not only an issue in or with the Islamic world. Also in a typical Western environment, books can appear on the market like the following one, claiming to be academic and about "Metal heads: Heavy Metal

Music and Adolescent Alienation", by an American professor called Jeffrey. As he calls his metal "objects" in his book in a quite pedantic manner with the first name, let us do the same concerning ours. If it appears inappropriate to address a professor as such, it should also appear inappropriate to address someone by his pet name who knows more about (metal) matters than the professor himself. But then the book is almost twenty years old now, and we can only hope that the time has brought wisdom. What makes this book a clear example of alienation by itself, is that it fails to explore a lot of important differences: between heavy metal music and metal music, between metal music and metal, between adolescence and metal (music), between adolescence and alienation and between alienation and metal (music) to start with. Others are to follow below.

In fact, a less problematic title would have been "American bourgeois: misusing metal music and academic funds by fearing critical dispositions towards societal customs". At the one hand, the author does his best to prevent himself from being associated with "heavy metal music and adolescent alienation", by telling he has only heard - I would not say listened to - a few free tapes, a few free shows and a few adolescents wearing shirts with metal logos, to respond shortly to his narrow questionnaire in exchange for a tape, for the sake of his "research" instead of any involvement. At the other hand, he talks about metal, and even more disturbingly metal music, as if he knows sufficiently what he is talking about. In this regard, he does certainly not count as an exception. The few valid lines concerning the music are either quoted, or valid in a small proportion. As I have indicated above, the more you know about metal, the more you would doubt though that anyone, including yourself, could just "grasp" what it is, and consecutively use it as a *passe-partout* for your own purposes.

What remains then are some American adolescents asked to complain for the book about their personal circumstances and public authority, to elaborate their suggested affinity with highly select illegal or morally controversial practices, and instead of making these distinctions and analyzing them: to blend it all into a profile waiting for the reaction: look here, how alienated metal heads are. If I asked for instance to middle-aged managers how many times they did not hire a critical adolescent metal head on grounds of the very same, if they were as honest, and if many responded that they go to the disco on Fridays, there would have been a likewise poor "finding" that disco music and discrimination by the settled go hand in hand.

Other than adolescence and alienation, Jeffrey utters (his idea of) high sensation seeking more often. However not really defined, and not clearly made distinct from the other two ideas, it is promoted as a core element in so-called heavy metal music. An example of high sensation seeking would be to drive faster than the legally allowed limit. Not only is it an odd strategy to talk about traffic, when one claims to talk about music. Also, most adolescent metal fans cannot even afford a (fast) car in the first place, and even the many older metal fans - quite overlooked in the book - seem to be concerned more about how their car can represent metal culture, by stickers of bands for instance, and to which destinations the car drives, by stickers of festival parkings for instance, where the automobile metal is considered cool by driving zero miles an hour. Furthermore, it does not explain why high sensation seekers can perhaps even more be found in house, techno and other genres from which most fans of heavy metal music explicitly want to keep a distance. On top of that, it does not explain why there are also a lot of low sensation seekers who are adepts of metal music. It has been my shop experience that the more quiet are even the "worst", by buying relatively more metal music, taking the artistic qualities more seriously, and more likely to neglect the red traffic lights because their mind is elsewhere than out of deliberate action. So, there are more grounds to think that the book is rather a display of high sensation seeking in itself.

The term alienation is very important though, we have to grant the author that. While I would not disagree that a lot of alienation exists, the question however is who or what is alienated when or where. If the author's alienated metal head "behaved", "integrated" or "conformed" himself more, this would not tackle the problem of alienation in the least. History should teach that, firstly, the dynamics of alienation exist much longer than the invention of metal music, secondly, alienation is much more related to directly or indirectly supported ideas of society as a whole which prove to be incomplete and alienating as such, than to this or that bunch of people within society alienated from that society. Of course, it is easier to present metal heads as some sort of aliens. Yet, this obscures the complication that in the first place society is some sort of alien, according to quite a few academics even in the Modern history of thought, which had better not be the end.

PS. This being said, I have commenced the process of songwriting for the new metal-based project Fireproof, which will pick up several elements of this treatise in a more artistic way... (This does far from mean that the art should be a mere means to any semantic end.)

www.ingramcontent.com/pod-product-compliance
Lightning Source LLC
Chambersburg PA
CBHW070939180426
43192CB00039B/2353